"a vivid collection _____ *ts about the savoir viv* _____ *a wonderful book abo* _____ *band."*

owen hatherley, author of red metropolis

"an essential, loving read for saint etienne fans — an exploration that's half sherpa tenzing in its commitment to the task, half sunshine girl in its loveliness."

jude rogers, author of the sound of being human

"how we used saint etienne to live beautifully negates the archetypal veteran band biography — forget tales of rock 'n' roll debauchery, this is a story of making memories and bringing dreams to life. ramzy alwakeel's analytical account is insightful and poignant, and this book is a timely, anti-nostalgic reminder of why saint etienne have such a special place in so many hearts."

hayley scott

How We Used Saint Etienne to Live

How We Used Saint Etienne to Live

Ramzy Alwakeel

Published by Repeater Books

An imprint of Watkins Media Ltd

Unit 11 Shepperton House

89-93 Shepperton Road

London

N1 3DF

United Kingdom

www.repeaterbooks.com

A Repeater Books paperback original 2022

1

Distributed in the United States by Random House, Inc., New York.

Copyright © Ramzy Alwakeel 2022

Ramzy Alwakeel asserts the moral right to be identified as the author of this work.

ISBN: 9781914420849

Ebook ISBN: 9781914420832

Printed in the United Kingdom by TJ Books Ltd

MIX
Paper from
responsible sources
FSC
www.fsc.org
FSC® C013056

Contents

do you remember how we used to live?

1.

They came from Croydon, and Windsor, and they came from London, and in a sense they came out of nowhere. Saint Etienne materialised in NW5 on the first day of the Nineties, which is the way it is when people start bands on the backs of envelopes.

Born at the advancing edge of what would later be called Generation X, Bob Stanley and Pete Wiggs had grown up together in more or less neighbouring suburban homes with three-day weeks and the occasional threat of war. They made each other tapes, watched *Top of the Pops* every week and collected psych albums. By the end of the 1980s they'd discovered electro and moved to the capital, where they set up a small record label.

Bob and Pete were sort of cute and very enthusiastic, but neither of them could initially play any instruments, which might not have been an issue had their new band not also lacked a singer. It was a relief, then, that Sarah Cracknell — whose childhood had been significantly more glamorous, thanks to her director father Derek Cracknell and actress mother Julie Samuel — materialised in the nick of time on the first day of the rest of their lives, and everything else wasn't so much history as an ongoing stream of now.

They had perhaps existed before all this as an idea. But the moment the calendar flipped to January 1 1990 was the moment Saint Etienne became theoretically possible — the start of the decade after history, the decade that arch Nineties pop historian Michael Bracewell would call a "temporal blender",[1] whose slippery essence of past as present and present as past the Saints would embody better than anyone.

---

[1] Michael Bracewell, *The Nineties: When Surface Was Depth* (London: Flamingo, 2002), p. 204.

That's because the thread that runs somewhat recursively through Saint Etienne's career is their relationship with memory, a relationship that informs both what they have produced and how they have produced it. They have sampled, catalogued, reassessed, reimagined and ignored the past. And while doing all this they have accumulated a significant past of their own, something they have accordingly fed through most of those same processes. This is a book about nostalgia, and anti-nostalgia, and modernism, and youth, and imagination, and the culture industry, and forgetfulness, and lists, and the resurgence of vinyl, and whether it matters if you were *there*, and whether there even was a *there*.

Saint Etienne are, in a way, well-known without being well-known. They have been successful enough as musicians, filmmakers and curators for more than thirty years, but outside of their active fanbase — and discounting for a moment the three or four medium-sized crossover hits they produced early on — they remain relatively obscure to the general public.

There are a few possible explanations for this. One is that their records and their presentation are so clever and self-assured as to be a little alienating, as though there's either a ton of assumed knowledge or some sort of private joke surrounding everything they do. Another is that they come across as too nice, too normal, not fucked-up enough, to capture the wider public imagination. A third is that being on an independent label hasn't afforded them the level of promotion and exposure that a major might have. But in truth, I still find it hard to understand why a band with so many bangers in their arsenal shouldn't have had a few more hits in a world where the KLF have topped the singles chart twice.

The KLF, the anarchic northern art school house duo who burned a million quid and dumped a dead sheep at the Brit

Awards, ran so Saint Etienne could walk. It wasn't a coincidence that both bands had members who'd been adjacent to the record industry in previous careers: both groups with differing levels of brashness traded on that insider knowledge by sampling and editing their way to brilliance, using the materials of recent history to create chaotic but compelling visions of the near future, bookish about music, lyrical about wax and belligerent about copyright, at least to begin with.

The KLF could certainly make a field full of people dance, but their primary purpose was to be pop's vanguard. Their escalating stunts and deliberate use of illegal samples were acts of libertarian defiance aimed at queering the music business. Saint Etienne, by contrast, positively luxuriated in the space the KLF had broken open, spying the opportunity to make records that had the spirit of punk and hip-hop but were almost embarrassingly gorgeous. In this sense, all postmodern pop owes Saint Etienne a debt.

Before long, the Saints were signed to Heavenly Records, the label founded by former Creation number two Jeff Barrett, and their 1991 debut *Foxbase Alpha* fused just about everything they could remember of the Sixties and Seventies and Eighties into something that could not have been made during any of them. Between 1993 and 1998, a period when British pop music was increasingly fixated on looking back, Saint Etienne were frequent fixtures in the top twenty, the *NME* and *Top of the Pops* with records that were of no time but their own. And yet they were so hip, so off-grid, as to be everyone's favourite secret, and thus they had their pick of collaborators: Kylie Minogue, the Manic Street Preachers, Étienne Daho, Aphex Twin, Andrew Weatherall. Because they were both the sound of the Nineties and the sound of time breaking down, it was never clear where they should be filed. They had the fuzz and freakout of Creation, Heavenly's distributor, whose signings included Primal Scream and My Bloody Valentine; they had the mysterious loveliness of the Cocteau Twins, the beats of Technotronic, the hallucinogenic ambience of the Orb, the wit of the Pet Shop Boys, the cool of Lush, the wall-climbing municipal desperation of Pulp. They had a small-time UK indie vibe but a global outlook. They were a bit psychedelic, a bit disco, a bit DIY, a bit dreampop, very English and unplaceably European, and probably everyone wanted to be them or shag them or both.

Because this is a book about Saint Etienne, it is a book about memory. Unfortunately, I was born in 1988, which means this is partly a book about things I don't remember, and means this history of how Saint Etienne used and created their own histories is partly a history of how I used Saint Etienne to create my own history too. And because it's therefore partly a book about me, we begin not at Saint Etienne's beginning, but at my beginning with Saint Etienne.

This is a personal history. But equally, because Saint Etienne are personal to so many, it belongs to all of us, even if names have occasionally been changed to protect the guilty.

For the avoidance of doubt, Saint Etienne are nothing to do with the city of Saint-Étienne in France, or with the actual saint, who is better known to English speakers as Saint Stephen. They in fact took their name from the football club, AS Saint-Étienne, and while they do at least like football, it isn't really what they're known for.

Their discography is similarly misleading. Saint Etienne did not release the album *Continental* on the continent. The title of *Good Humor* really is spelt that way. The sound of water cannot be heard on *Sound of Water*. The members of Saint Etienne have what you might call active imaginations. If I want to understand this pack of jokers, they are the last people I should ask.

The first people I should ask are the ones who put them on side four of *Now That's What I Call Music! 33*.

Primarily, that's because *Now 33* is where my own Saint Etienne history began, but it also happens that *Now* compilations were at that precise moment the most reliable thing in the world. They were a pump from which I would wager everyone who liked pop music in the Nineties drew water at least once.

There was all the Eurodance you could eat. There were two Oasis songs on one album, one D:Ream song on two albums, one-hit wonders and comebacks and slight returns and whatever else they could clear the copyright for. There were these slightly lame gags in the running order — stuff like "I Want Your Love" coming before "I Don't Want Your Love". They were value for money, and they were so much more than that.

They were out of date within weeks, their unsold copies gathering dust in motorway service stations where it is always late afternoon on the last Friday of the summer holidays, but for once it would not remotely be a cliché to say that they were the soundtrack to our lives, at least for the generation that will always expect to hear "The Universal" after "Father and Son", "Another Night" after "Saturday Night", "Freedom" after "Wannabe" and so on.

There is a joke in here somewhere about pearls and swine, because *Now That's What I Call Music!* took its cartoon pig and weirdly literal name from a 1920s bacon advert. Only after appearing on five albums was the pig benched in favour of a jazzy logo that was made up on the record covers to look like a shopping bag and a Filofax and various other things people might have thought were cool at a particular point in history. (Some people think bacon is cool, but the pig had been wearing sunglasses and seemed to have a record collection, which confused the issue of whether it was edible.)

Then suddenly the logo was in the sky. On the bottom of a pool. Briefly the logo was nowhere at all. Then it was in complex 3D environments. There were mountains, cities and deserts. There was snow and gold and, in the case of *Now 33* itself, enormous Perspex numbers hovering stupidly above a vast lake.

For better or worse, these were the circumstances under which I "discovered" Saint Etienne.[2] However many albums they release, it always feels appropriate to talk about Saint Etienne as though no one else knows about them. They are mischievous and foreign like that. They're an erotic novel found in a museum bookshop that you can't read because it's in Portuguese.

No one ever has the biggest hit of their career with the bonus track from a singles collection. No one except the Etienne, anyway, who took "He's on the Phone" all the way to number eleven in late '95. This was a big enough success that the song scraped onto *Now 33* as part of an inspired if slightly mad run of songs at the end of the album, for which seemingly all the weird stuff had been saved up.

I was one of a statistically insignificant number of children who felt it was important to listen to compilation albums without skipping anything, so to make it all the way to track thirty-seven gave the song a precarious ritualistic wonder, like

---

[2] Sort of. See below.

seeing the sunrise after staying up all night. But there was no daylight here. "He's on the Phone" sounds like a November night in a posh hotel where you don't belong. It is the reflection of neon signs in a wet pavement afterwards, a taxi ride to anywhere — no, I have nowhere to go, but please just drive.

Though every decision within its relatively minimal universe sounds supremely intentional — a woman caught between two lives, a wicked rush, a record that tips from luxury into despair just as Sarah Cracknell sings the words "got the cash" — the song was actually sort of an "Accident". Saint Etienne had recorded its low-key original version, under that title, as part of a collaboration with continental cult favourite Étienne Daho (like a French, Eighties version of Leonard Cohen) in 1994. "Accident" largely sank without trace. But not quite, because it made its way into the hands of pop mastermind Brian Higgins. Recognising its potential, Saint Etienne had asked him to rebuild and remix the track so they could release a new single for 1995 without actually having to record anything. So far, so St Et, except that doesn't explain how it ended up so perfect, because in speeding it up and putting a club beat on it Higgins brought out something enchanting and desperate.

All the same, accidental perfection is their modus operandi, so "He's on the Phone" was exactly the right track to promote Saint Etienne's first greatest hits album, *Too Young to Die*. This was, you have to admit, a pretty odd title for a band who weren't breaking up. Though I knew next to nothing about Saint Etienne, I had evidently read its name while studying the small print inside *Now 33*, because it chewed away at me for twelve years until, for some inexplicable reason, I dreamed about it one night at university — a fictional version of this album whose real front cover I had never seen, stacked inside an imaginary record shop that I can still picture because I remember it so often (I think it was derived partly from Tower Records in Piccadilly Circus and partly from the Boots in the main concourse at Leeds railway station) — and woke up feeling like, if I could only get hold of it, then who knew what other dreams I could make real?[3] The Lord, who presumably likes the Saints, works in mysterious ways.

"He's on the Phone" arrived in Saint Etienne's laps after three albums and five years. Here at last was the song that would launch them into the medium-time. The world was within their grasp. They could have rushed into the studio and made a whole album with Brian Higgins. They could have borrowed D:Ream's strategy and pointedly re-released each of their old songs until something got to number one. But of course, displaying an instinct for self-sabotage you can't help but admire, they followed it up with silence. Bob, Pete and Sarah would put out no new material for three years, cancelling the planned release of a single in 1996 and disappearing into Europe.

A clue that the Etienne were approaching this crossroads had already come in the form of their last studio album before the hiatus. Compared with its predecessors, *Tiger Bay* was suspiciously bucolic. It didn't sample any films or TV and its cover art was an oil painting that didn't feel very zeitgeisty because it was from 1856. Scandalously, it didn't even have an essay on the back, the first and only time they omitted to include a literary roadmap with a record.[4]

---

[3] This story looks ridiculous written down, but honestly it did happen.

[4] There were no sleevenotes because there was no time to

When they resurfaced at last, in 1998, they were in Sweden with an album (*Good Humor*) that sounded like rollneck sweaters, exposed wood panelling and fresh coffee. It was like "He's on the Phone" had never happened.

This was the first of several midlife crises through which they would drag their willing fans, but for all the left-turns their career has never faced backwards.[5] No rehashes. No "I Love the Nineties" tours alongside Robson & Jerome or whoever. Maybe because Saint Etienne never wholly committed to us but always had one foot out the door, hiding behind bricolage and quotation and their own wit, they seemed to get better, richer and more intriguing with each reinvention. Unlike basically anyone else who materialised around the time they did, Saint Etienne made their three best albums in the twenty-first century. They may not have sold as many records as their peers, but they have been making music entirely on their own terms for three decades. They've even done it without killing each other.

Perhaps it would be more accurate to say that I had *rediscovered* Saint Etienne through *Now 33*. I already knew, in the vaguest possible terms, that they existed. The first time I'd seen their name on a record cover had been slightly prognostic: their hit "You're in a Bad Way" had also been track thirty-seven (honestly) on a different compilation album, *Smash Hits 1993*, bought by my mum at the end of that year to keep me occupied, ostensibly a purchase "for the whole family",

---

commission them; for financial reasons, Creation was in a terrible hurry to get the album in shops before the end of the 1993/94 tax year.

[5] Don't think about this metaphor too much.

though I think she probably just meant "for the good of the whole family", and in any event I don't think it ever left my room. The branding was sort of irrelevant because the same people — Ashley Abram and Box Music — were also behind the much bigger *Now That's What I Call Music!* series, and obviously (correctly) had the Saints down as a kind of "side four" band even at this point.

I wasn't old enough to understand "You're in a Bad Way" properly and I didn't really think about Saint Etienne again, whoever they were, until "He's on the Phone" came along. All the same, my five-year-old brain did its best to crunch the song's various lyrical clues into an image of mediocre early adulthood that persists even now when I think about what it will mean to be "grown up", though I am now older than they were: someone's older brother with a badly knotted tie and a thousand-yard stare boiling the kettle after getting caught in a storm. When I picture the early Nineties, what I really see is a soup of telly and billboards and pop songs, imagined memories all flowing into each other like rain-soaked hair dripping into lukewarm coffee in a bedsit. In other words, I *don't* remember how we used to live, but I *do* remember "How We Used to Live", and for that matter *How We Used to Live*.[6]

From here I can pretty clearly see you recalibrating, chewing your fingernails, adopted northerner, cross-legged on a bed in an attic, writing essays about Autechre and dreaming about every year of the last two decades at once. There is a picture taken of you sitting on this bed, during this summer, looking up

---

[6] The Saint Etienne film, not the vintage Yorkshire Television educational series, which recklessly I have not watched despite indirectly naming a book after it.

at something you've blu-tacked to the wall. I don't know if you know you are being photographed. Do you know I am writing a book about you? As prone as you are to self-mythologising even at this age, I think I go unnoticed as I rifle through your head and your surroundings, mind-reader that I have grown to be. But as "He's on the Phone" begins, the final track on the album you bought because you had dreamed about it, I see you exploratively doing the same thing to our eight-year-old self, the opening hook a countersign that dissolves the student bedroom covered in posters and ticket stubs and sends you back to the small room in your parents' house where you first heard it. And as you look through the kid's mind you realise, I realise, that each time he played that song he was semi-consciously trying to piece together the incomplete world that might have produced it, a universe built from songs and TV and fragments of adult conversations all distilled and filtered through a pre-adolescent brain.

It's never totally been clear to me quite why Saint Etienne sound like going on holiday, but here's my theory: going on holiday is easy to remember. Not the postcard images, so much, but the disordered mental snapshots. The queues for airport parking, the view from the window of a coach, the family arguments, the sunburn, the wet feet, the smell of the home to which you eventually return at night, forgetting to turn the water back on, all of it shot through with heightened emotions, higher stakes, higher prices. Saint Etienne sound like take-off, but they also sound like finding perfection in the imperfect. That's why I remember being you, sitting on the bed in 2008 after getting dumped. Isn't it all still somehow slightly fabulous, they asked you from the early Nineties. You felt like shit but you had to agree.

Long before I started thinking about any of this, Saint Etienne were digging through their own memories and record collections like indie magpies. In the beginning, they made albums like they had made zines at school, cutting sampled dialogue with the names of paving companies, in-jokes with childhood photographs, baseball cards with football stars and celluloid pin-ups. They repurposed beats and strings and voices, covered the classics, painted their faces into a Victorian canvas and a Kraftwerk photo, stamping their irreverent humour on forgotten futures and alternative histories of London and Europe.

Then they began creating their own stories and traditions. There were the festive freebies (gigs, singles, albums — no band since Saint Etienne's youth has made such a relentless fuss about Christmas). Instead of rummaging through the BFI archive for films to chop up, they made their own. Instead of sampling other people, they sampled themselves. Eventually, they wrote records about their own records. Their music was played in actual cinemas instead of imaginary ones. They published endless sleevenotes to append to the original sleevenotes others had once written for them.

Pop music has always been used as a tool of invention and fantasy, but Saint Etienne are perhaps unique in understanding that the rewritten present necessarily becomes the rewritten past.

And always, hanging over their perfect songs, the question of what it *means* to remember — how remembering and archiving can alter, improve, degrade or even replace the source material.

Always, too, the question of how it could be beautiful, and amusing, and sometimes sad, to think about these things. Saint Etienne can be as sincere as the best of them *because* they are so often playful. Likewise, it is somehow funny when they accidentally produce a minor hit single, even though *Too Young to Die* is track-for-track one of the finest collections of hits, minor or otherwise, ever released.

A worthy successor to "He's on the Phone" finally came along in 2008, so fashionably late that thirteen years had gone by. The song that might have made Saint Etienne's name for a second time had the uplifting title of "Burnt Out Car". In its high-intensity melodrama, it sounded quite a lot like "He's on the Phone" with more bottom end, but lightning rarely strikes twice and this time the track failed to chart, irresistible though it undoubtedly was.

"Burnt Out Car" was also quite weird. It sounded like Sarah was being interrogated in a nightclub about a murder and why she wasn't wearing any earrings, but I think I got lost in the beat for a second and maybe I misheard her. It was, because why not repeat the formula, a slow song that had been sped up and remixed by Brian Higgins, long after the Etienne themselves had given up on it, not even bothering to release the original, save on a demos album in 2006, by which time it was already a decade old. Actually, Higgins had a couple of goes at sp(l)icing it up — one in 1997 before really nailing it in 2008. So far, so St Et, except that doesn't explain how it ended up so perfect.

There is a joke on the back of an early Saint Etienne album that the group do not exactly hide their light under a bushel, and while they are obviously a bunch of clever sods I'm not sure I otherwise agree. "He's on the Phone" was a hit by accident, "Burnt Out Car" wasn't a hit at all, and loads of their other best songs are almost wilfully obscure, released only in Japan, only in America, or only by mail order.

Saint Etienne won't go out of their way to come to you, but from a band of crate-diggers this is hardly surprising. By putting out records that you can only buy at gigs, online, in different countries, on the sixth Thursday of the month, etc., they're encouraging us to discover and explore them in a gradual way that was once the norm but hardly still exists in the digital age. You have to be paying attention. Saint Etienne reproduce the way *they remember* discovering music: at car boot sales, on market stalls, under the counter, through fanclubs and clubnights and word of mouth, by being in the right place at roughly the right time. I think they know we like it like this. Not so good for those of us who weren't in the right branch of Our Price in 1993 or whatever, but there'll be something else along next Christmas.

A distribution strategy like this has another effect. By making themselves so collectable (thirteen of their full-length releases could be legitimately described as limited or obscure, which is more albums than most bands release at all), the Saints also encourage us to curate and archive our own personal Saint Etienne histories, just as they collect and sample and compile the records they remember from theirs. They force us to repeat the way they used music. They expect us to index our memories by their songs, to attach this or that record — a foreign pressing, now dog-eared, or lost, or missing a cover — to a book, a fling, a night out, an art degree, a day spent bunking off school so we could buy an import single, memories that are sometimes (we hope) more authentically us than the lives we now find ourselves leading n years later. It's clear from the way they write songs and write *about* songs that this is how they experience the world, though — as full-time musicians — they've probably been able to stay a little truer to those ambitions than the rest of us.

This conundrum is the subject of a song from 2012 called "Haunted Jukebox", which describes the way your favourite records can buckle under the weight of all the memories they accumulate. The final track on the group's eighth album, *Words and Music by Saint Etienne*, "Haunted Jukebox" was an obvious winner: a jangly staccato arrangement holding up an aching melody that ripped off the band Bread (I think unintentionally) and a lyric about first love lost.

Words and Music was the Saints' first album release since I'd become a fan and thus the first one I'd had the pleasure of hearing when it was new to everyone, not just to me. Unfortunately "Haunted Jukebox" was rather more directly personal than I had expected because the day it came out was also the day my boyfriend was moving to Japan (to make matters worse it was the same boyfriend, now rehabilitated, who'd dumped me that time before, just after I got into Saint Etienne). It was a relationship built almost entirely on music — we'd met in the lending library for records and CDs that he once ran above Leeds University Union — and so basically every record I'd ever listened to reminded me of him. "I can't escape, I'm sure you know," the song went, "in Purley Oaks or Tokyo" — I mean, *come on* — "it goes much further than our tune, when every record in the room, they leave me haunted." It was outrageous and I listened to it on repeat for weeks, and while I cry at lots of pop music it's no exaggeration to say I cried at "Haunted Jukebox" *a lot*.

I suppose Saint Etienne already know this. They knew a thousand indie nerds would hear themselves in this song about pop music functioning as external memory, and moreover that the song would become a memory of its own as 2022 rolled around.

In a couple of ways, *Words and Music by Saint Etienne* was a coming of age, partly because they put it out twenty-one years after the release of their debut, and partly because, over the course of its thirteen tracks, they came of every age they had ever been. The premise was straightforward: a record about pop music by three people who really loved pop music. But it was also a record about Saint Etienne, even if that wasn't their express intention, about the way *their* words and music have shaped our lives, and the lives of the band itself. It was an account of growing up with pop songs and growing into pop stars, just anonymous enough that it could have applied to any of us with delusions of grandeur but with enough of the personal that we knew, for once, this was largely their story.

Words and Music for me will always feel inseparable from the 2012 Olympics. The most straightforward explanation for this is that it came out a couple of months before they began, and that I was by this time working on a local newspaper in east London. This meant I was unavoidably having to think a lot about the games — struggling through Iain Sinclair's analysis of the balance sheets in *Ghost Milk*, reporting on parochial admin dramas and watching Stratford being rebuilt — at the time the album dropped.

But it also feels like there is a political link between the attempted rehabilitation of Britain's toxic national identity through the child-safe social democratic stylings of Danny Boyle's opening ceremony and the commercial rehabilitation of a band so English and so London-centric as Saint Etienne, whose lot had been near-total obscurity for the preceding decade. None of their albums had made the top forty since *Sound of Water* in 2000 and even the involvement of hitmakers

Xenomania, the outfit founded by Brian Higgins, hadn't been able to reverse their fortunes. Around the time I got into them, the Etienne seemed less than ever like a band anyone you met might feasibly have heard of. But *Words and Music*, in a way that seemed to reflect the liberal mainlining of pride in England and London in this year of the Olympics and whichever jubilee it was, ended up being their most successful album on the British chart since the Nineties.

Of course, you only have to scratch the surface to understand the fallacy of thinking like this. Though they didn't share Iain Sinclair's abject scepticism, Saint Etienne had been relatively wary of the Olympics when London first made its bid to host them, documenting the already neglected areas of the Lower Lea Valley that would subsequently be lost to the stadium and "village" in their second feature film. More to the point, the Saints had long ago stopped being a band that made the kind of hagiographic records about London that they first became known for.

To be honest, if there is one myth I want to dispel with this book, it is the notion that St Et simply write about how great the capital is all the time. They have certainly propagated this myth themselves at times. There are three members of the group and it is natural that they have differing opinions on this subject from each other, some of which you will see in the following chapters. But, to put it bluntly, Saint Etienne are not some sort of musical arm of the Greater London tourist board.

Bob, Pete and Sarah were children of the Home Counties, and so London was both their creation myth and their rapture. They were painting it onto the sides of caves before language. But they were visitors who became locals, and the way they regarded the capital became less simplistic the more time they spent with it.

All their changing feelings about London had begun to crash into each other around the turn of the century. The result, not long after, was *Finisterre*, which is for my money St Et's magnum opus, as well as kind of their second midlife crisis. It's an album of warnings from history. It's the reaction of a band who have learnt that their early visions of this city were partly built on propaganda, and who are trying to work out which bits can or should be salvaged. In that sense, the record isn't exactly negative — there are moments of real beauty and a spirit of hope pervades much of it — but it's not what you'd call romantic, whereas romantic is exactly what you'd call their first couple of albums.

And yet, more than any other Saint Etienne project, *Finisterre* dreams desperately about the future, about the London that young people might build from the rubble: collective, creative, fluid, kind, a place where the most vulnerable are secure. "I feel a nostalgia for an age yet to come," announces Michael Jayston halfway through side one like a transcendental newsreader. "This time we're gonna find a way, find a way to get away," sings a hopeful England World Cup squad (1982) at the very end of the record.

Maybe it isn't a coincidence, given all the above, that *Finisterre* was the moment the Saints' commercial fortunes temporarily began to nosedive, the starting gun for ten lonely years in search of an opening ceremony. At the time of writing, though, Saint Etienne's course has been on the up since the Olympics, with a high-charting studio album in 2021 and a film festival at the BFI the same year.

Things are yet to get better for everyone else at the sharp

end of London, either locally or globally, and heretically I don't think this is something that can be fixed using pop music.

But maybe pop music is the soundtrack to praxis. And if there hasn't been a whole lot to look forward to besides the progressive death cult of late capitalism, then — bearing in mind that idiom about remembering history or being doomed to repeat it — there has at least been the reliably unreliable drip drip drip of Saint Etienne's reappearance every three to seven years, each time reminding you to look back and look forward, and each time reminding you of the last, and of the first, and perhaps most crucially of *your* first.

do you remember how we used to remember?

2.

Saint Etienne have been making and faking history in their own way for more than thirty years.

And if we want to tell the story properly, to understand how they first tangled memory up with Memorex then began to unravel it, then (just this once) we need to go back to the start.

That's because the ideologies that shaped their first two albums — *Foxbase Alpha* in 1991 and *So Tough* in 1993 — could be said to have left their mark on everything that followed.

It could even, perhaps, be said that everything that followed was a memory of these original exercises in memory. But we're getting ahead of ourselves.

My mum didn't buy records very often when I was little, presumably because she was busy.

For some reason, though, I've never forgotten the ritual that accompanied them: she would record each LP onto tape straight off the bat, right the way through, generally as soon as we got home from the shops, without even a dry run to check for defects, which I suppose meant my mum and the C90 got the same first pass at the music, their memories as blank as each other.

Probably she just wanted to make a clean copy of the album before the grubby, curious fingers of a three-year-old could examine the playing surface.

But perhaps the reels captured some ghost in the machine, too, a memory of what the music sounded like before it became familiar.

At roughly the same time as all this, Bob Stanley is doing something similar with a cassette machine on the other side of the Channel.

It's a Saturday evening in 1990 or 1991, and Bob's tuned

the radio to a long-wave sports station, where — he hopes — veteran football reporter Jacques Vendroux is about to say the name of the French Ligue 1 team AS Saint-Étienne.

Since Saint Etienne is also the name of his band, Bob reckons it would be funny to put a recording of this moment at the beginning of their debut album.

But each time he presses the "record" button, he knows only that this *might* be the take that becomes an indie classic. Equally, he knows it might just be one of Vendroux's tangents, a segment that he'll be winding back and taping over in a couple of minutes with a sigh. Every recording he makes is a record of his own not knowing.

Suppose this is the one. Right now, Vendroux knows even less than Bob. He is unaware that the next forty-three seconds of his broadcast will be the only ever totally live performance of "This Is Radio Etienne", the track that will land more or less unedited at the start of *Foxbase Alpha*. Imagine the pressure. Every pause, every intonation, echoing through dance music history at 1.875 inches per second.

Fortunately, Vendroux hasn't been briefed. He believes the words coming out of his mouth are his own, little realising he is someone else's soloist, an honorary Saint for one night only. Forty-three seconds of fame. When Vendroux finally says "Saint-Étienne" with the tape rolling, it is the punch-line to a phonographic joke he doesn't know he is telling, in a language Bob will never get round to translating. "This Is Radio Etienne" is a machine with its own ghost, a memorial to not knowing — a record of two men who are respectively unsure and unaware that they are making a record. Is it obvious? Perhaps every new Saint Etienne fan gets one shot at hearing it like this before the waveform collapses, before the script and the timing become familiar and the track for them too becomes a memory instead of a discovery.

Collaging past and present

Three-quarters of a minute isn't much in the grand scheme of things but, when you're listening to a low-quality recording of a sports commentary in French, the seconds do mount up.

The Saints would rarely leave the tape running for so long. While making those first two albums they showed a clear preference for much smaller fragments of audio, s(p)licing up other people's work like questions in a general knowledge round: a few seconds of this, a few seconds of that, a bassline, a quote from a film, a handful of notes from a soul singer.

Considering the legal hysteria and extortionate price tags attached to sampling in the early Nineties, this was a bold strategy — especially given that Saint Etienne didn't actually clear all the material they used on original pressings of *Foxbase Alpha*. They were the KLF's better-looking younger siblings, and they knew it.

Rock music history tends to pinpoint the origin of sampling in the 1940s, in the emergence of *musique concrète* and its use of "found sounds". But I would suggest going further back, to the peripatetic folk music collectors of the early twentieth century who travelled the country and the world trying to "capture" the traditional songs of different cultures using emergent recording technologies or the best they could approximate through notation — because, if they weren't actually mixing these songs and sounds together, then they were nonetheless beginning the industrial process of placing music from one context into another that was ill-equipped to understand it.

Sure enough, raids on the work of Black and indigenous performers would prove a goldmine for white DJs and record execs in the Nineties, a racialised extension of those projects from decades earlier.[1] But hip-hop artists like De La Soul, Public Enemy and the Beastie Boys had been doing it in reverse, sampling existing hits and, in the case of the KLF, literally setting fire to money.

It was in the latter tradition, whether through innocence or design, that Saint Etienne emerged, not so much collectors as vandals. They stole from the rich. They deterritorialised music and film by saving the wrong elements of it — never the hook or the chorus of a song but some odd piece of instrumental or half a line from a verse, fragments of dialogue that didn't make sense on their own, blasts of sound distorted by low-quality kit and everything pasted into their albums like scrapbooks while other musicians put their plundered treasures behind glass. An educational record about decimal currency was chopped up so it sounded like someone's aunt trying to sell drugs. Key scenes from *Peeping Tom* and *Billy Liar* were reduced to meaningless outbursts between tracks. It was like they were making ransom notes from whatever they had to hand.

---

[1] See, for example, Ryan Diduck, "All Play and No Work", *Fact Magazine* (2019), <https://www.factmag.com/2019/05/15/moby-play-20-years/> [accessed September 6, 2021]. Before Moby's *Play* there was Enigma's "Return to Innocence", which didn't generate a penny for its indigenous Taiwanese vocalists until they sued its producers; German New Age group Sacred Spirit, who based a top ten album and an international hit single entirely on indigenous American peoples' chants and dances; and so on.

Bob: The samples on *So Tough* started out being favourite lines of ours from films — mostly from films, bits of TV, a few interviews. They ended up being almost entirely British films and TV because American stuff was impossible to clear, even then. It was kind of the peak of paranoia about people sampling and getting away with stealing other people's songs or work, when the fees that companies were charging were briefly astronomical.

It was really just cutting up and collaging our favourite work, and giving a thumbs-up on record to people that we liked — we were big Madness fans, and Soft Cell as well. And obviously British kitchen sink cinema too, so there are bits of *Billy Liar*, *That'll Be the Day*, a film called *Made* that starred Roy Harper, and *The Family* from 1974, which was incredible, pretty bleak, the first reality TV show in Britain.

Pete: The way we approach most things stems from the way we used to do fanzines. We used to do silly collages for each other just to make each other laugh, and tape compilations and stick bits in between — we'd always do that. It's probably just informed the way we work in general. We'd take comics and cut out bubbles from one comic and put it on another. The *Radio Times* — we'd do that cut-up sort of thing, change all the descriptions of programmes and things.

Apart from "This Is Radio Etienne", which came straight off a live broadcast, most of what St Et used as building material in the early Nineties was old. The TV shows were repeats, the films were black and white, and the singles were second-hand. But the effect wasn't at all dated — the samples, though they were recognisably drawn from decades gone by, were cut up and strung together in a merciless way that invoked turntablism and tape edits (and, for that matter, daytime programming and FM radio) more than classic cinema or soul records.

The way Saint Etienne refract glimpses of the past through the lens of the present is kind of how it feels to be an adult remembering childhood. This isn't a coincidence. Children are useful metaphors in the Saints' story because childhood is when we believe most strongly in magic, and because children are modernists — they represent the existence of a future. (When Richard X and Saint Etienne remade *Foxbase Alpha* track "Like the Swallow" in 2009, they got children to sing what had originally been Sarah's vocal, which made it sound like the song had gone backwards and forwards in time at once.)

They blurred past and present in other ways, too. St Et's breakthrough hit in 1990 was a cover of "Only Love Can Break Your Heart" by Neil Young, a waltz originally released when the Saints *were* children, its bones broken and reset into a shuffled 4/4 beat and given a piano house makeover so chic and aching you knew it must have cost virtually nothing to make. Saint Etienne love covering songs in new styles: they released three more as singles between 1990 and 1993, and their fanclub albums included charming if unusual takes on classics dating back to the Fifties. But half the time their own songs had a quality that was older than the old stuff — you'd probably (wrongly) have guessed that "Spring" and "Hobart Paving" were covers, because it quickly turned out these self-professed amateurs were actually among Britain's best songwriters.

To complete the effect they used their record sleeves as a sort of revisionist time travel, alienating and immortalising images originally created for entirely different uses — paintings, news photography, family snaps, library pictures. Inside the cover of *Foxbase Alpha* they reprinted more than two dozen photos of film and music stars from the Sixties and Seventies; they later put the album's deluxe edition inside a giant Subbuteo figure painted with the 1970s AS Saint-Étienne strip. For *So Tough*, instead of putting a band photo on the front like a normal group might have done, the Saints decided on a Seventies polaroid of Sarah at the age of six: an image shot by her father around the same time as the Beach Boys released the album *So Tough* was named after.[2]

In short, the Saints' first two albums are an overlay of every decade in the second half of the twentieth century, film and half-inch tape stuck together by the same idle hands that made those fanzines. Bricolage was their homage. To the Britpop bands on the rota for the *NME* cover around the same time, having an eye on the past meant actually trying to *be* the Beatles or the Kinks, but Saint Etienne — who loved the Sixties and Seventies as much as anyone — mostly came out sounding prodigiously and obnoxiously current.

Bob: It's always annoyed me when people say we're retro because I really don't think we are. We're always conscious of making something that sounds like it's been made in the time it's been made, because what else are you going to do?

Borrowing the best parts of the past but living in the moment and creating something new from them — that's modernism. At least, that's my definition of modernism.

---

[2] Theirs was called *Carl and the Passions* — *"So Tough"*, which is a copyeditor's nightmare.

There are maybe twenty identifiable samples of film, TV and other spoken word sources in the skits on *Foxbase* and *So Tough*, as well as the sampled breaks, vocals and instrumentals used in the songs. By the time of *So Tough*, the group was paying more (in the region of £35,000) to license copyrighted work than it had otherwise cost to make the LP.

One reason for all the sampling was simply their *desire to use samples*: they were heavily influenced by hip-hop and electro, by De La Soul's *3 Feet High and Rising* in particular. Another was the fact that they wanted to share their favourite recordings with people. And sometimes it was just a quick way to get hold of sounds that were otherwise out of their reach, like the warbly string and flute voices produced by the Mellotron.

Bob: I've always been a record fan, ever since I was a kid, being taken to my parents' friends' houses and looking through their records, imagining what they might sound like from the sleeve or the label. I've never particularly been into live music. I've always loved studio sounds, studio creations, rather than a live sound.

All the ideas would have come from our record collections. We'd have just adapted a bassline from somebody else's record, adapted a guitar part, a rhythm guitar part. Even the echoes and reverbs — I remember we were listening to *What's Going On* and saying we really wanted to get that kind of reverb on "Mercy Mercy Me" on the percussion, almost like a sonar, and we had no idea how it was done. We'd just mess around with a cowbell and reverbs and echoes until we had a close approximation. We had a Roland Space Echo. That was a lot of fun.

The idea of sampling films and TV just came from not wanting to be secretive about our influences, I suppose. In fact it was the opposite — wanting to acclaim our influences, which were sometimes the Beach Boys or someone fairly obvious, or someone more obscure. It's not like David Essex was getting many critical plaudits when we sampled *That'll Be the Day*. It's just an extension of who we are, I suppose, and if our lyrics aren't necessarily very autobiographical then those clips are, which is a slightly oblique way of telling people about your life without it coming across in the lyrics. It's just saying who we are and what we love, and trying to share. It's as simple as that.

In a sense, Saint Etienne's work was an unwritten manifesto for the collective ownership of sound, an audio commons, because a lot of what they nicked hadn't been entirely original to begin with.

The Mellotron sample on "Spring" is a perfect example. This esoteric keyboard instrument had been particularly beloved of British bands in the Sixties, and it was from an album by one or other of these that Saint Etienne lifted its distinctive analogue sound. But the Mellotron itself was a sampler, albeit a primitive one: its keyboard was patched to a collection of physical tape loops hidden inside the casing. When you pressed a key, what you heard was a tape recording of the corresponding note, played by a session musician at some undisclosed point in the past.

Beats and breaks are another example. You might recognise the drum pattern on "She's the One" as a sample of "Being Boring" by the Pet Shop Boys. But "Being Boring" owes its rhythm to one of the most sampled performances of all time: Clyde Stubblefield's famous solo on James Brown's "Funky Drummer". So whose work, exactly, were Saint Etienne using?

That question is even trickier to answer when you consider

that, like any samplers or synthesisers, the Mellotrons and drum machines were already extracting value from the session musicians whose labour they had replaced each time they were used.

Saint Etienne were, basically, DJing with history the moment they began to write music, pre-empting the likely fact that their records — and with them all the decontextualised primary texts with which they were cut — would in turn be used in ways they had no control over: played on dancefloors and in living rooms and bedrooms, remixed, sampled, lent, borrowed, copied.

Bob: My method was basically to find a song structure I liked from an existing song and break that down, work out why it works. The verse would be a certain length, the bridge, middle eight, whatever. The chords might be from a few different records.

But I'm not a musician. I can't sit down and play piano or guitar so all I know about is my record collection and other people's records. In that respect, it's always borrowed. It's borrowed from various different sources.

Pete: We'd have some soul records and we liked the chords from them — we couldn't sample it but we would work out what they were and copy those and sometimes it'd be like, well, we like the bridge of this song, that's alright, the verse of this song, the chorus of this one, and shall we see what happens if we put those together? And sometimes it would work in a weird way — 'cause we didn't know music theory then — sometimes you're not supposed to jump from that chord to that, but we were like: "Oh, that sounds good, let's do it", and Ian Catt would be like: "You can't do that! You can't do that!"[3] But Ian's skills were crucial to those early records and he was accepting — occasionally bemused, perhaps — toward our approach, unlike the prevailing rock mentality of the majority of studio people we encountered in those days.

This modular way of repurposing music would culminate in *Tiger Bay*, Saint Etienne's third album, which lifted melodies from European and American folk songs and fused everything together with modern electronic arrangements. It was the closest they came to "folk music collector" territory. But Saint Etienne weren't a band that made anyone rich, and *Tiger Bay* perhaps ought to be seen in the context of the Saints' treatment of *all* music as folk music, their position that all sound belongs to the commons. In other words, who can claim to have written a melody that is truly their own?

Maybe the understanding that *everything* is sampling, that all music and sound have existed on a spectrum of shifting ownership since the first notes were played and the first words spoken, that authorship and subjectivity are borrowed, is how they became such good songwriters, knowing exactly how to combine and manipulate tunes and emotions, when to be disrespectful, when to nick stuff and how to get away with it.

It's not that the Saints have ever meant to offend anyone by behaving like this. It's just that they've never recognised

---

[3] Ian engineered and played on *Foxbase* and most of the band's subsequent records, and is sort of a fourth member of Saint Etienne — joint fourth, anyway, alongside long-time backing vocalist Debsey Wykes, manager Martin Kelly and filmmaker Paul Kelly.

authority — their own included. Hence the profane streak in Bob and Pete's sleevenotes for their "found" recordings of themselves, the rarities and demos they dug out of carrier bags and released as fanclub albums throughout the Nineties and Noughties: "Horribly unfinished", "from the sublime to the sub-mental", "a new insight into our sick English minds", "ham-fisted dirge", "bad design", "music that could never be listened to", and so on.[4]

That's why tracks like "Spring" and "Nothing Can Stop Us" have as much right to classic status as any of the recordings they drew from — not just because the Saints wrote their own tunes and lyrics over them, nor because they came out sounding so beautiful. They're classics specifically because the act of collaging all those pieces of history was a raid on the territory occupied by copyright lawyers and rules about music. Bob, Pete and Sarah were mavericks, but their songs were so lovely that it was easy to miss.

Records

If you grew up when Saint Etienne did, and if you liked music, record collecting was simply what you had to do — less a hobby, more a necessity, even a way of life. Records were *serious*.

And so even when the business of crate digging changed thanks to the internet, and thanks to the waning popularity of wax, Bob, Pete and Sarah wanted their singles and albums to be used the way they'd used their own favourites: to create

---

[4] Incidentally I've long suspected with no real basis that *Foxbase Alpha* is somehow derived from the words *foxtrot alpha* — that is to say, the letters "FA" in the phonetic alphabet.

communities and forge friendships, to signify subculture and status.

Sarah: I remember getting "Ghost Town", the Specials, and I know that was a kind of known song but when it first came out it wasn't so much — it took a while for the Specials to catch on. I was really young and my friends didn't know anything about it. And I was a massive Felt fan. There were about five of us and we were really obsessed with Felt, we loved them. I had this old Citroen 2CV — you know those kind of French cars with the funny eyes at the front? — and I used to cram us all in and we'd drive around the country going to see Felt. But it felt like a little gang. There's nothing like a little gang, is there? It's great having a little gang.

Pete: Something like *Forever Changes*. It created a picture in my head of a world and then, having learnt more about the band afterwards and seeing that really good film about Love, their existence was a bit more grimy, I think, and druggy. It's got a sort of bucolic feel to it and just a sort of fantastic thing that, as a sixteen-year-old, I created all these images to, in my head, that probably were quite different to the ones that were in the band's minds at the time. The first time I heard Love, Bob had put "Andmoreagain" on a compilation cassette for me and I was on holiday with my family and had a Walkman. Just saying the title of that puts me in the back of that car, listening to that, cutting myself off and being blown away.

Bob: When a new record came out and it was somebody me and Pete both liked, which was quite a lot of the time because our taste was pretty similar, it was always exciting to take it home, put it on and listen to it together, and sit there basically in silence, waiting till the end of the album and going "well, that was great" or "that was terrible" or whatever.

I borrowed the *Head* soundtrack from the Monkees film and we listened to that and it completely blew us away because the film hadn't been shown on TV at that point — the film hadn't been shown anywhere since it was first screened in 1968. The soundtrack was a complete collage and was a huge influence on our first two albums, and you had no idea what the film was like, so that was an exciting moment. I remember listening to it in Pete's mum and dad's house in Croydon, just trying to imagine what on earth the film could have been like. It just sounded so entirely abstract. And when we did see it eventually, it was pretty abstract.

I eventually found my own copy in a shop in Lincoln. I've been to Lincoln twice in my life and they had that, and it was six quid, which was cheap even then, and I remember on the wall in the shop they had the Bakerloo album, which was a boring blues rock album on Harvest which I would have had less than no interest in. But I remember thinking it's funny that those albums from that period look so evocative even though I thought the music was terrible. It had a line drawing of men working on a railway, a Victorian line drawing, and the font that says "Bakerloo" was in orange on this black and white sketch, and basically that's what the *Tiger Bay* artwork was based on, as it looked so involving to me — I think we even used the same font.

I remember that was the same day I bought *Head* in the same shop in Lincoln, and the Bakerloo album was forty quid. Oddly precise memories — it's funny how your brain does that. I can remember those details of one trip to Lincoln when I was twenty-one and probably hungover because I would have been out with my mates at college the night before but it sticks in my head. I bought a really nice Crombie the same day.

Because memories like these were so important to them, Saint Etienne consciously or unconsciously found ways to help other people replicate them. They set up a fanclub. They piled in-jokes into everything. They released flexi-discs and slightly dodgy Christmas records. And they continue to elude fans with this or that limited edition: a bonus disc, a Record Store Day release, or the exclusives that appear year after year on the world's lowest-capacity website (Saint Etienne's online store has crashed dramatically every Christmas for a decade). They believe there should be no record without an acquisition story and no song without a memory.

In a way, then, what I've really been trying to figure out since I started this project is: do I remember the first time I heard "He's on the Phone"? Do I remember the first time I *remembered* hearing "He's on the Phone"? And: am I afraid all these extra layers of memory will hide the ones buried further down, as if the song weren't already laden with enough baggage while tiptoeing out of that hotel room?

There are two answers. Yes, it's true there's more to remember than there used to be. But it's also true that each of these memories is partly a memory of the earlier ones. It isn't so much that the original impression has gone dark — it's more that it's been split apart. I no longer only remember it as it was: I also remember the memory. Maybe a bit of the detail is worn away, but memories of pop music aren't about detail, are they? They're about the flash of indescribable bittersweetness that survives however many times it is felt. I might not remember the first time I remembered, but that memory is echoed — somewhere — in all the other memories I have.

And while some of the memories in the middle have faded (because it would be insane to remember every one of the hundreds of times I've heard that song), plenty seem to survive for no clear reason. My record collection is a patchwork of mundane flashbacks — bedtime, a Tube journey, a skipping disc, the smell of a shop. Maybe our brains decide what memories to keep based on how often we think about them or the emotional state we associate with them. Maybe these were all profound experiences of art, even though they now feel arbitrary to me. Is it nostalgic to think about them? Is it moving? And is that why Saint Etienne's first two albums are also a patchwork of mundane flashbacks?

Collaging, but without samples

The influence of *Foxbase Alpha* and *So Tough* stretches through Saint Etienne's work. Their short attention spans and level structures, modernisms that equated the sublime with the ridiculous, were mission statements.

Given the eye-watering costs and legal headaches involved, what the band couldn't keep doing was using other people's records to achieve that mission. They needed a cheaper way of doing it.

Fortunately, Saint Etienne had realised early on that they could recreate the abrupt chaos and maximalist appetite of sampling in the way they wrote and edited, without actually using any samples at all.

One of their first attempts at this was a track called "Fake 88". Perhaps the Saints felt they'd slightly overdone it, with its meticulous representation of mischievous, anachronistic memory, because "Fake 88" was abandoned after completion, finally limping out in 1993 on a various-artists compilation. (It had been intended for greater things, though: Saint Etienne wrote it to go at the end of *Foxbase Alpha*, which would have made an already good record quite a lot better if they'd only held their nerve.)

"Fake 88" starts innocuously enough. Its first half is a sultry, echoey ballad that seems to have the bassline from "Whole Lotta Love". Just as the energy picks up with an arpeggiated harpsichord figure, the track is saturated by a tide of noise that sounds like a train pulling into a lake. At 2:23, as the reverb and the waves ebb away, a totally different song begins. There's a little waltz played on a solo electric organ. Then there's one of the strangest cameos of all time, from former Duran Duran bassist and future Robbie Williams songwriter Stephen Duffy, who materialises a few seconds into the waltz and starts narrating "a scene from a film circa 1982":

> We drove down George Street en route for Wendy's.[5] Glen Campbell was on the radio singing a song about cleaning his gun and dreaming of Galveston. "What's this?" she said. "It's Hall and Oates or nothing for me." Of course, this was pre "House Nation", and I asked her: "What is anyone going to remember this decade for?" She paused for a second, then said...

---

[5] Perhaps believing the song to be more famous than it actually was, the *Croydon Advertiser* would speculate in a 2017 article ("19 Songs Which You Probably Didn't Realise Mention Croydon") that this was a Wendy's branch in Croydon, where there is indeed a George Street.

After hesitating just long enough for the backing track to completely change direction again, Stephen's unidentified companion answers the question in verse, reeling off a mood board of clothes, haircuts, politicians, soap stars, magazines, scandals and singers. (By way of illustration, one small segment of the list goes: "Mark King slapped his bass/ and early issues of *The Face*/ Sigue Sigue Sputnik, Margaret Thatcher/ Toto Coelo and *Spycatcher*.") It runs for more than a minute, during which its timeline becomes completely disordered, like the imperfect memory that it represents. And at the end, Stephen's own character replies as though in a dream, which of course he is: "I don't remember any of that. If you can remember the Eighties you weren't there."

Sarah: I have the worst memory, Pete has the second worst memory and Bob has the best one. I do think that there is a thing that you remember the good stuff, obviously, and your brain is designed to put the bad stuff to the back of it somehow. Some people think we're nostalgic and I think we are to a degree, but I don't like that nostalgia where it's like: "Oh god, it was so brilliant in the past and now's so crap." It's about remembering, celebrating stuff, but things have moved on and that's natural and it's as it should be.

"If you can remember the Eighties you weren't there" is an odd thing for someone to be saying in 1982, but that isn't the kind of detail in which "Fake 88" is invested.

The track is a monument to the chaotic misfiling of memory in the videotape era. Look out for: Nik Kershaw, whose breakthrough was in 1984; *EastEnders*' Dirty Den, whose first screen appearance was in 1985; Stephen's own stage name Tin Tin

Duffy; and a load of references to people Bob and Pete went to school with. Stephen doesn't mention 1988 once.

Its canonisation of the everyday is as curiously moving as it is silly and, through the rapid cuts in its script, "Fake 88" seems to anticipate the head-spinning way samples are strung together on *So Tough* more than it reflects the slightly lumpier tape work on *Foxbase Alpha*. In it too is a blueprint for Saint Etienne's future more generally, this weird, humorous memory of looking forwards ("what is anyone going to...") with an altered recollection of the past ("...remember this decade for?"), a poet's catalogue for no museum that exists in physical space.

Things that don't matter: whether Stephen Duffy's character is actually meant to be Stephen Duffy; whether the scene takes place in 1982 or 1988 or some other time; whether "I don't remember any of that" is a lie; which branch of Wendy's. You don't need to understand everything Stephen says to understand "Fake 88", just like you don't need to know where all the skits and references come from to understand *Foxbase* and *So Tough*; in fact, it's better in both cases if you don't. The obscurity of Saint Etienne's sources is an act of future-proofing because now and again you stumble across the song or the film or the Wendy's where they got an idea or a sample and see them in a whole new light, the same feeling as when you realise you've been hearing a lyric incorrectly for half your life. No coincidence that they don't print lyrics in their albums.

They tried the "lists" technique, toned down, in a couple of other songs around this time. Sarah read out a load of place-names in the middle of 'Girl VII', and namechecked pieces of popular culture (Chris Eubank, the KLF, the *Racing Post*) in "Mario's Cafe". But "Fake 88" is by far the most unruly of the three, and the song whose rather bizarre form is most clearly dictated by its contents. I wonder if this is why it was binned from the *Foxbase* tracklist, whether it all seemed too silly once the novelty wore off.

With hindsight, though, "Fake 88" was an important track. For one thing, it prefigured the Saints' film career, a medium in which it already seems a lot more natural to cut quickly between shots. For another, its theme of unreliable memory would resurface repeatedly in Saint Etienne's work.

The imagined past

I said Saint Etienne materialised on the first day of the Nineties, but in a sense they were born the day Bob Stanley and Pete Wiggs heard the Monkees' *Head* for the first time. Their imagined idea of "what on earth the film could have been like" is a dream processed through flashbacks and record shops, a real memory of a false memory whose pursuit left its mark on every song they made.

On some level, this Fake 68 must also have been the experience Bob, Pete and Sarah were trying to recreate with *Foxbase Alpha*, their own *Head* whose samples and references would inspire equivalent imagined ideas for people to chase through record shops and railway stations in other cities. *Foxbase* perhaps wasn't so much a document of the specifics as a general synaesthesiac splurge intended to be morphed into a confected, abstract vision of a time and place that plenty of its listeners would never have seen. After all, the Saints knew they were making records for the future. And so I find myself asking: what on earth could Camden in 1991 have been like? Croydon in 1982? Is that why Stephen Duffy calls it "a scene from a film"? The itemised list of Eighties paraphernalia in "Fake 88" describes a particular world of pop stars and soap stars and waffle cardigans, Fake 82, Real 91, overdubs on a mental multitrack. But are any of the mental pictures accurate? No doubt people who were actually there would find it weird that anyone should want to concoct a Fake 95 or 93 or 91 or 88 or 68 at all.

Bob: The Eighties started amazingly and ended amazingly and the five years in the middle were just an absolute desert — high Thatcherism and, you know, everything that could be horrible was horrible. You were absolutely treated as an outsider if you didn't go to a nightclub in a suit and tie. By 1989, that was completely over.

The way the Eighties get treated by younger people, by indie revisionists and by vaporwave or whatever, I find really fascinating, because it was a grim time to live through for a lot of people.

Saint Etienne developed their style and techniques around the principle that the past was not a utopia. In other words, the irreverence wasn't just about samples; the cheeky way they used recorded sound was only one of its consequences. The bigger picture has always been the Saints' refusal to valorise things just because those things happen to be old. They do not recognise the obligation to respect one's elders.

But they liked things on their own merits. They liked the way old records and films felt and sounded. And they liked collage, and the textures that were created when they cut things into the middle of their albums.

Since none of this required the recordings they used to be genuine classics, the Etienne eventually hit on the idea of replacing all those costly samples with things they'd recorded themselves, pieces of audio made to sound like they were sampled from other places even though they weren't, like time-travelling to nowhen.

The origins of the Fake Sample can be traced back to 1991, specifically to the chorus of "Girl VII", where the Saints looped a clip of Sarah singing a few ambiguous syllables as though her voice was something they'd found in a box of old records. But it wasn't until the turn of the century that the Etienne began insourcing their own found sounds with any regularity.

If normal samples are ways to memorialise, reimagine and future-proof the past, the Fake Sample is a blank memory, a cipher, a way to remember remembering without a source — a sample of itself, Foxbase Omega, a cancelled denominator, the flipside of those imagined memories of 1968 and 1988 and 1995, which are constructed partly from reality but have no physical presence. The Fake Sample has physical presence but no reality.

Its moment came in 2002, on Bob, Pete and Sarah's sixth LP *Finisterre*, as a direct result of Saint Etienne branching out into cinema. Alongside Paul Kelly and Kieran Evans, they made a feature film to promote *Finisterre*, covering twenty-four hours in London, sunrise to sunrise, its hazy shots of bustle and weather narrated by the English actor and voiceover artist Michael Jayston. And as a means of foreshadowing the movie, which wouldn't actually be released for another year, Jayston also recorded twelve spoken-word skits for the album itself. A handful of these Fake Samples would subsequently be dubbed into the film to give the impression that the Saints had sampled their own cinematic work in advance, like they were *Billy Liar* on *So Tough*.

Some of Jayston's lines for the album are masterclasses in comic delivery — like when he recites, with gravity, the title of the Phil Ochs song "The World Began in Eden and Ended in Los Angeles". Some of them deliberately sound like they were snipped from larger pieces of work: "I have news — good news from Notting Hill. The consignment of white gold has arrived for Mr Anderson." These are not samples except perhaps in the sense that every recording is a sample of the world — but they sound and feel like samples because of their form and treatment, the way they drop abruptly into the LP without context and without warning, like the speech bubbles in the collages Saint Etienne used to do on paper and on vinyl.

Perhaps as a homage to sampling itself, a flex to show they could still run the process in both directions, *Finisterre* does also contain a number of real samples as head-scratching as anything on *So Tough*. Most are towards the end of the record. Indeed, the very last sound on the album is a clip of the 1982 England World Cup squad performing "This Time", their official song for that year. (England did not, of course, win the World Cup that time, or for that matter any subsequent time, but the song memorialises a state of not knowing, a bit like "This Is Radio Etienne".)

The star here, however, is Jayston. Not unlike Stephen Duffy on "Fake 88", his preposterous script and deadpan delivery hit a sweet spot, just silly enough and just profound enough to be endlessly quotable.

Another reason for the overall success of the project is that the Saints' Wagnerian decision to script and record the majority of their own samples effectively elevated both the movie and the record into simultaneous cult classics because of the way they referenced each other.

It was also inevitable. Bob and Pete had originally sampled their way to proficiency, making instruments out of scissors and tape. That instinct subsided for a while, which was good because it didn't add £35,000 to the bill every time they went into the studio. But if you leave scissors lying around, someone will eventually cut themselves.

The Fake Album

Saint Etienne love a hiatus. And in the years that followed *Finisterre*, the new commitments of their families and their filmmaking kept them busier than ever outside the studio. They once went the best part of a decade without putting an album out, and when you work at that rate every release is a reunion.

I claimed earlier that Saint Etienne's career had never faced backwards. Except, by 2017, there was nowhere else to look. That's because Britain itself was facing backwards, or perhaps more accurately up its own ass, increasingly obsessed in old age by its imperial past, not as a source of shame but as a sort of weird arcadia. And so the album Saint Etienne released that year, *Home Counties*, was a Fake Album, the Fake Sample's logical conclusion, because the present itself was fake.

Home Counties' cover art shows the house in Croydon where Bob Stanley grew up. It looks like the sort of high-contrast stock photography that made Stylorouge's designs for Blur so recognisable in the mid-Nineties. But the picture is new — a quotation of nothing, an original with the aura of a forgery. Ditto the stickers on the front with their quirky flower power typeface, bearing messages like "records are your best entertainment value" as though it was 1967 and the album was in mono.

This goes on inside the record cover, where there are lists of people convicted for "recent criminal incidents" in different counties around London: theft of a funeral wreath, shoplifting, arson, Essex, Surrey, Kent. Alongside them is a photograph of Timperley Court in Redhill, annotated by little kitchen sink stories about its residents: lonely hearts, favourite bands, disputes about road maintenance. It's quite likely they were all made up, because some of them are a bit ridiculous and because real people get funny about being immortalised in print. But it's plausible enough that they *could* have been real, or at least based on reality, like the pasts we all imagine when we hear certain records.

The sense of not knowing whether things are as they seem is the key to *Home Counties*. The album's first track, "The Reunion", consists entirely of an accurate reconstruction of the opening sequence of *The Reunion*, a show on BBC Radio 4 that reunites the surviving key players from a piece of history. Pretty much the only clue that the whole thing is a Fake Sample rather than an actual recording of the radio is the fact it begins with the words "This is Radio 4" (rather than "BBC Radio 4"), which is perhaps *slightly* too perfect a callback to the title of "This Is Radio Etienne".

"The Reunion" is a reconstruction of *The Reunion* but also a reconstruction of sampling generally, especially a reconstruction of the first time Saint Etienne sampled the radio, way back at the beginning of *Foxbase Alpha*. What's more, *Home Counties* may not be *The Reunion*, but it is still a reunion. And so, even if it's a lie, it's kind of true.

Opening the album with this simulation gives what follows a slightly nightmarish edge where you never fully trust what you're hearing, particularly when a real sample of BBC Radio 2 staple *Popmaster* turns up on track eight. *Home Counties* almost feels like the simulation of a Saint Etienne album, the dummy LP in a production where Bob, Pete and Sarah play themselves.

Maybe the point of this record wasn't so much to look back as to demonstrate the hollowness of looking back. Saint Etienne described *Home Counties* as their Brexit album — and whatever you think about the European Union it's fair to say the official Leave campaign attached a lot of importance to simulating a past that had never really existed, anything complicated or problematic completely airbrushed away. This kind of fetishism is the total opposite of the iconoclastic, hands-on way Saint Etienne had originally used images of the twentieth century.

Amusingly enough, *Home Counties* was also the group's first release on cassette in the UK for twenty-one years. Could there be a metaphor more apt? The revival of this barely supported format was the music industry's version of bringing back blue passports, an infantilising retreat into a value system where the quality of "good" is superseded by the quality of "old".

The storylines on *Home Counties* are awash with claustrophobic small-town imagery that seems to find only partial release in the album's final songs, "What Kind of World" ("this is our home, but I don't feel at home") and "Sweet Arcadia". The latter is a paean to moving out of the city, to the people — especially those in the inter-war years — who sought a better life beyond the poverty and smog of London. But its sprawling, ghostly arrangement and Sarah's spoken-word delivery seem to underline the sinister modern-day parallels in its lyrics: "We took your land," she says dispassionately at the end of the album, "and we made it our land." It's not obvious whether we're meant to feel victorious or dispossessed.

Home Counties has a *Black Mirror* uncanniness, like suburbia, like a memory lapse, like the version of Britain offered up by the Leave campaign (or, to be honest, the version of the EU offered up by the Remain campaign), like buying cassette tapes in 2017. There's something horrifying about the reflection it holds up to a country so obsessed by nostalgia that it can't see the present. It is the only Saint Etienne album that doesn't feel modern. Perhaps they needed to make it just to remind everyone.

Remembering the present

Few would have predicted, when *Home Counties* came out, that Britain would soon be looking back on 2016 and 2017 as years of relative normality. At the height of the Covid pandemic, music was the furthest thing from plenty of people's minds. Plenty more of the people who worked in the industry — musicians, venue staff, record shops — were unable to operate. Some lost their jobs. And of course, worse than that, some of them lost their lives or their health or their families and friends.

One of the consequences of the collapse of routine, though, was a collapse of expectations. Tours had been cancelled. Bands who'd been midway through recording albums had to abandon them. The vacuum created a lot of time and space, albeit privately, for musicians who were more or less unemployed to process what was happening around them.

And so it was that Saint Etienne, who had themselves been halfway through making a record when lockdown began, ended up making a very different kind of album only months later, one that probably would never have been made at all without the plague and the curfew.

I've Been Trying to Tell You landed in shops after three lockdowns. It was an unusual Saint Etienne LP — unusual for its brevity (it tops out at eight songs); unusual for the fact it was made without the Saints ever actually being in a room together; and unusual for its relative lack of vocals. The album has perhaps one chorus, and a lot of ad libbed lines in isolation, and that's about it.

But the most unusual thing of all was the fact it was built almost entirely out of samples — real ones, rather than fake ones, more even than *Foxbase Alpha*. *I've Been Trying to Tell You* is really an ambient hip-hop record in the spirit of the Avalanches or DJ Shadow — more, anyway, than it is a pop album.

Saint Etienne's career had by this point gone on so long that sampling songs from a quarter of a century ago now meant borrowing hooks from the Saints' own contemporaries and even successors. Dusty Springfield's 1967 recording of "I Can't Wait Until I See My Baby's Face" was twenty-four years old when the Saints sampled it for "Nothing Can Stop Us" in 1991. Mind-meltingly, the Lighthouse Family's "Raincloud" was the same age in 2021 when St Et used its bassline on "Fonteyn". Can that be right?

Pete: I just thought it'd be a good challenge, microscopically pulling things apart and seeing what you can do with repetition that still keeps the attention — and quite trippy, I suppose, as well. For me it was fantastic, the time it came, in terms of the lockdown — we were allowed to go exercising once a day, that was about it, and the weather was amazing so in the morning I'd go for runs in the greenery, and I'd never done that before working on music, so it was a weird time and I'd really thrown myself into this. So it's not like it was about lockdown, but it was an amazing escape just getting lost in these tracks.

Sarah: I feel like the samples were a tool to put across our own feelings and our own idea for the album. A vehicle to put across our own thing.

It's a strange way to memorialise lockdown, using material from the late Nineties and early Noughties, but it's also the only way Saint Etienne could ever have done it. *I've Been Trying to Tell You* doesn't really sound like the end of the twentieth century any more than *Foxbase Alpha* sounds like the Sixties and Seventies. Both albums use the past in a way that could only be contemporary, the products of circumstantial limitations overcome by technology.

Pete: There's some geeky software developments, things that we couldn't have done thirty years ago — or five years ago. There's some new software where you can pull apart samples, which I used a lot on this, so you can take the drums and bass out of a sample and make them into separate tracks. When we started making music, the sample technology had come down in price. You would have had to be Trevor Horn or something — massive Fairlight samplers cost forty grand each — but suddenly making these records was within our grasp. It was kind of the advent of the new technology around that period that meant we could do that, so I thought, well, this new stuff around now — take advantage of it and see what creative possibilities there are.

I think of it more as almost archaeological, imagining I'm digging through these relics from a period and trying to find some sort of essence that was in there. It was a deliberate policy to slow everything down and I'd often change the key of the track as well to find something that I thought was more moving.

Meanwhile, Sarah's vocals on *I've Been Trying to Tell You* are as ghostly and unsettling as the unintelligible loop on "Girl VII", right from the first line she sings on the first track, "Music Again": never had a way to go? A wait? A weight in gold? A weighted goal? It's like she's singing in another language, or maybe it's more like we don't understand English, just like we didn't understand once-familiar surroundings after the pandemic came.

Sarah's voice all over this record has the formless form of the Fake Sample, which is pretty much the way she supplied it, recording on her own and sending the results to the others to work into the music. *I've Been Trying to Tell You* is the bridge between Saint Etienne now and Saint Etienne then, because on no previous St Et record have the two been muddled up like this. If anything, the Fake Samples make it sound more like a memorial to the Saints themselves than to anything external, a premonition of how St Et could sound in the future when other people in turn sample these records.

Saint Etienne have built a kind of second-hand novelty into *I've Been Trying to Tell You*, much like they did using the samples on *Foxbase* and *So Tough* — except that the treasure hunt is backwards, because this time the album is the solution rather than the clues.

The source material isn't buried like Easter eggs across popular music and film history, but within the record itself. Most listeners, probably by now of a certain minimum age, will already know or half-know the songs it samples, things like "Love of a Lifetime" or "Beauty on the Fire", so the novelty doesn't come from recognising them in the wild but from recognising them in captivity the way Saint Etienne use them, hidden in plain sight — slowed down, split apart, looped, bitcrushed, they become instruments in themselves.

The treasure hunt is the same when it comes to the Etienne lyrics quoted in the film, also called *I've Been Trying to Tell You*, that accompanied the album. These days you start off knowing the answer but have to find the question.

Like calling a track "This Is Radio Etienne" thirty years earlier, the immediacy in the title of *I've Been Trying to Tell You* seems to defy the expected charge that this record is "retro", a work of nostalgia for a pre-Covid era. But I wonder if any of that era has bled onto the tape in the original samples all the same, a memory of what the music sounded like before its essence was isolated, or invented, before it became unfamiliar — a memory of *knowing*.

In this regard, the Saints have returned to the place they started off, memorialising ways of hearing sound that differ from the ways they and we now hear it.

As we've seen, the way Saint Etienne learnt to create collages, to cut up the world and stuff it into their music, to disrespect their source material just enough that they could get away with it, to transform the old into the new and to question authenticity, has kept cropping up in their music, their films and their artwork.

But the story isn't complete. Even when you thought you'd untangled it, somehow there was something of the unsettling spirit of sampling that remained in everything they did, even the songs that didn't contain lists, that seemed to be *just normal songs*. The memory and the tape still bore imprints of each other.

do you remember the way we live now?

3.

Spotting the samples was straightforward until the Saints got cocky. You used to be able to tell that any given sample in a Saint Etienne record was a sample because of two things.

The first thing was that the sample was alienated from the track around it — the product of a different mind or a different history. It had a sound that made it an outsider in the sonic space. Its words, if it had words, didn't fit into the song's narrative. Or it had a different arrangement, from a different time. It was crackly. Or it dropped abruptly in and out of the track like someone opening the wrong door.

As a result of the first thing, the sample also had an alienat*ing* effect on the listener — a quality of taking *you* out of the track into its own space, the other side of that wrong door, either because you knew the song or film that had been sampled, or because you didn't. This was the second thing. Together, these qualities might be referred to as the *sample-ness* of a sample.

But by the late Nineties, Saint Etienne had figured out that they could recreate the otherness and disruption of samples with their music and storytelling, that those disorienting flashes of recognition or bafflement could come from their choices of words or even the way a track was mixed.

The Saints' approach to other people's records in the early Nineties was also their approach to the worlds that their music drew from: folk memory and folk who forget, smoking areas, dreampop, the roar of the road, the roar of the crowd and do you believe in magic, daytime TV, shopping centres, English weather, football training and the train lines that joined everything up. Saint Etienne were able to extract from these the same qualities that they could extract from old recordings or films. Other bands might have drowned in these worlds, or become part of them, but St Et — perhaps because of the way they had first learnt to work — managed to keep it all at a distance, critical, spatial or emotional. It's the same distance you feel from a sample that takes you out of the familiar space of one track into another, or into nowhere. It's a surprise that comes from somewhere you thought was safe.

What I'm *not* saying is that Saint Etienne's lyrics are alienating by virtue of being fake or unrealistic, or that their music is unfeeling because it is clichéd or overcooked or awkward. Rather, the way Saint Etienne reproduce distance is by skewing and dissolving pop music's traditional, often somewhat confessional, subject/object relationship between singer and audience in a way that can be jarring and confusing even while it's still thrilling and enveloping.

The overlapping language of music and movies makes it easy at the best of times to slip sideways from revolutions per minute into frames per second and back again, but I think this love affair with distance is why you can never talk about Saint Etienne without someone mentioning film at least once, because filmmakers know exactly what it means to frame and present a world without ever belonging to it. Often it's in the group's own sleevenotes that the anointed writer brings up the fact Bob, Pete and Sarah make pop music that sounds like moving pictures, but it isn't just about the evocative instrumentals or the fact they literally do keep writing soundtrack albums. Plenty of pop stars can be dramatic but something about Saint Etienne's entire project is *cinematic*.

It's standard, for example, for Sarah to say things like "split screen" midway through a lyric, for the Saints to open their albums with scene descriptions: "Milan, when I was a kitten", "A redwood tree, the radio, they moved in down the hall", "Rays of light upon the counterpane". The chorus of "Hug My Soul" is like someone blocking a scene: "I'll be there to run into your arms." There's the eponymous "Postman" observing "silhouettes at the window" like David Attenborough crouched in a suburban garden; songs with filmic titles like "Pale Movie", "Action", "Shower Scene", "Dilworth's Theme"; the lyrics to "Burnt Out Car" — how many other singers are so committed to the visual that they would muse about hair dye for an entire verse?

Sarah: I grew up on a lot of film sets and going off on location. Such a charmed life! And I used to love it. The location stuff was really great fun but I used to love all the stuff at Pinewood Studios. You would go in these massive hangars and there was a certain smell of heat and dust, big lights everywhere and cables all over the floor, and it was always like: "Shhhh!" You had to tiptoe and try not to trip over cables and things like that. Film was a huge part of growing up.

Then there's the way so many of Saint Etienne's protagonists carry on in the second and third person.[1] "He's on the

---

[1] A few years ago, music tech writer Dimitar Bankov analysed the word use in 237,662 sets of song lyrics and concluded that the first-person singular "I" made up close to 7% of all the pop (7.44%), electronic (6.99%), rock (7.04%) and alternative (7.16%) lyrics in the dataset. See Dimitar Bankov, "Statistics: Most Used Words in Lyrics by Genre", *Coding in Tune* (2018) <https://codingintune.com/2018/04/09/statistics-most-used-words-in-lyrics-by-genre/> [accessed September 13, 2021]. While writing this chapter, mainly out of curiosity, I did something similar, running the lyrics for the Saints' two most successful British albums, *So Tough* and *Tiger Bay* — the records that put them on *Top of the Pops* and magazine covers and, importantly, whose lyrics could more or

phone, and she wants to go home." "All of his friends have been wondering why he spends so long with her." "Toast is burnt, and your coffee's cold, and you leave all the post 'cause it's nothing but bills again." "She wears sad jeans, torn at the waistband." "I heard she drove the silvery sports car along the empty streets last night." (Well, OK, there's an "I" smuggled in there.) "She thought she'd look good in purple jeans." "Boy is crying." There isn't a single "I", "me" or "my" in key Etienne songs like "He's on the Phone",[2] "Mario's Cafe", "Pale Movie" or "How We Used to Live".[3]

What's more, when Saint Etienne *do* appear in their own

---

less be entirely deciphered — through a specialised word counter (https://planetcalc.com/3205/). This revealed that the word "I" appears ninety-six times across the two records, which is about 3.76% of all the lyrics they contain. Similarly, the word "me" makes up 1.72% of *So Tough*'s lyrics and appears just once on *Tiger Bay* (in the line "she said, 'I wish that he'd just left me'"), but represents 2.96% of pop lyrics in the musiXmatch dataset that Dimitar used, 2.71% of electronic lyrics, 2.41% of rock lyrics and 2.19% of alternative lyrics. Finally, the word "my" represents 1.41% of lyrics between the two albums, compared to 1.97% of musiXmatch's pop lyrics, 2.05% of electronic lyrics, 2.05% of rock lyrics and 1.94% of alternative lyrics. Incidentally, while cleaning up the lyrics to run through the counter, I expanded all the abbreviations to match the way the musiXmatch database "reads" songs. In other words, the ten times Sarah sings "I'll be there" in "Hug My Soul" all count towards the twenty-eight uses of "I" on *Tiger Bay*. The more you know.

[2] Unless you count the "je" spoken by Étienne Daho in the French-language middle eight.

[3] Aside from the ad libs at the very end.

songs, they do it either merely in passing or not in the first person at all. The who's who in the verses of "Mario's Cafe" is fairly obviously a list of actual people the Saints used to go to the caff with, so it's easy to picture the real Bob, Pete and Sarah around the plastic tablecloth. But could the "Saturday Boy" in the song of the same name be a young Bob or Pete, chatting up girls at non-league football matches? Might any or all of the members of Saint Etienne have cried when Maurice Gibb died, or bought vintage Subbuteo catalogues off eBay, like the character of Johnny in "Teenage Winter"?

Even when Sarah sings in the first person, she kind of sounds like she's reading someone else's lines. One way or another, it never really seems like *Sarah Cracknell* is the one fighting with her sister Sylvie, locked out in Fortis Green or telling anyone to "lose that girl".

Remembering the present — again

Techniques like these mean Saint Etienne often become liminal figures in their own records, unseen intermediaries between the action and the audience. This isn't unheard of — think of "Eleanor Rigby", "Dedicated Follower of Fashion" or "Country House" — but it's a step away from the more direct tradition of lyrics like "I feel love" or "last night I dreamt that somebody loved me". Saint Etienne's records engender a kind of instant nostalgia, not because they are "retro", that word Bob hates, but because they build absence into their *now* so that we miss it even while it is happening. Their records embody a sadness without object, sometimes because of the untouchably perfect soundscapes that make us feel like we are watching the silver screen rather than anyone's reality, sometimes because the lyrics themselves keep us at arm's length by being cryptic, and sometimes simply because of Sarah's ice-cool delivery.

The best example of the three coming together is *Sound of Water*, their part-ambient part-acoustic millennial pivot from Scandinavia to Berlin, and the album where more than any other they really nailed being strange and lovely at the same time.

Saint Etienne have always used space and geography to tell emotional stories — remember what they can do with a seafront or an urban clearway — but by *Sound of Water* and its companion, *Interlude*, the spaces were imagined, the computer-drawn scenery in the artwork as real as the missing sound of water. "Walk the street as it becomes a river and the cars are shining in the morning sun." "Over the coastline, just like pebbles on a shore." "Palm trees, the sound of Karen Carpenter." These are dream sequences, the present faded like an overexposed photograph or a childhood memory. On these records, Sarah is an instrumentalist, not just through her voice but through her words, like the internal narrative of the music itself brought to life.

Except, well, you just can't make out what she's saying sometimes. Like I said, Saint Etienne have never printed lyrics inside their albums — except for *Continental*, whose Japanese-only release included the Japanese record industry's customary bilingual transcript and equally customary transcription errors (the "hypothermia girl" in "He's on the Phone" being a particular favourite) — and Sarah's vocals are so often obscured in the mix that there are whole lines I can't decipher. She delivers the languid postscript to "How We Used to Live" at the end of *Sound of Water* like someone walking away from you as they talk, "up the riverbank and over the viaduct", her words disappearing under the piano and the rhythm and eventually, fugue-like, under themselves. "Keith Emerson"[4] does the same thing at the beginning of the album, fighting to be heard over the crowd noise as he announces "we're gonna give you *Pi-* we're gonna give you *Pi-* we're gonna — we're gonna give you *Pictures at an Ex-* we're gonna give you *Pictures at an Exhibition*" — perhaps St Et's way of telling us that we won't actually hear water on this record, just like Mussorgsky's images exist only in the mind.

Sarah: I have absolutely nil ego when it comes to a piece of work, a song or a track. For me, it's all about the end results. If it needs lots of me then I'll do lots of me, and if it needs none then that's fine and, if it needs a little bit here and there, I'm fine with that. I really just want the end result to be as good as it can be and as it should be.

My delivery can be quite detached — not always, obviously, I do mean it! I can sing in a slightly detached way if I'm singing about things that aren't me, and then I might get to the emotional bit and feel more in the moment. The vocal doesn't always have to be the focal point. It can drop in and out because it's not, just at that point, the most important thing. The words aren't the most important thing — it's the feeling and the mood. Elizabeth Fraser was one of my favourite singers and it's very much for that kind of

---

[4] This is actually a Fake Sample of Nathan Bennett from the band Bridge & Tunnel *pretending* to be Keith Emerson, but I don't think you can tell. The recording is a very good reconstruction of Emerson's now-famous opening line on Emerson, Lake and Palmer's live album *Pictures at an Exhibition* — their prog adaptation of the tone poem of the same name by Russian composer Modest Mussorgsky.

reason: she's not necessarily singing real words most of the time. It's not about the words — it's about the feeling.

Saint Etienne impatiently synthesise the effect of fading memory without the need for any time to pass at all. They present the present the way the rest of us remember the past. They stand so far away from the action that the emotional detail is lost, as if to time. Sometimes the words go missing in the texture of the song. Other times it's because Etienne songs are either so poetic or so full of specific geographical and biographical reference points that you don't know unless you know, like faces and names surrendered to amnesia — Purley Oaks, World of Twist, the skin that smelt just like pebbles.[5] Who or what is Suzie Banana Stand? Sometimes, even though Saint Etienne really do have nothing to do with France, *they do things in French*, just to mess with you, like the lovely but inscrutable "La Ballade de Saint Etienne", like "This Is Radio Etienne", like the Étienne Daho collaboration *Reserection*, right the way back to the fact they called themselves Saint Etienne in the first place. And to top it all off, you can't even be sure if you're hearing Sarah or someone else half the time: Debsey Wykes, Moira Lambert, Donna Savage, Sarah Churchill and Natalie Imbruglia drift in and out of Saint Etienne songs. In some cases, the guest vocals are obvious,

---

[5] Pete: "I remember I'd split up with a girlfriend I'd been with for like eight years and we were playing 'Like a Motorway'. That was one of her favourites and she's kind of mentioned in the words — the 'skin smells just like pebbles' bit was based on this foundation she used to wear, just this daft comment that I threw in there. But we did a gig and I just burst into tears on stage. No one saw, I don't think."

like Q-Tee's mesmerising drawl on "Calico", but in others the difference between Sarah and Not Sarah is a little blurry, like it's *Mulholland Drive*. And honestly, like chasing memories, it's a fool's errand trying to solve each mystery as it crops up. Enlightenment doesn't lie there. Far better to let the record's abstract logic wash over you, exactly the way you wouldn't with a singer positioned dead centre of the stereo field asking you to love them.

The fourth wall

Turnpike House was built in the mid-Sixties as part of the King Square Estate between Angel and Old Street in north London.

Appropriately enough, Saint Etienne's 2005 album *Tales from Turnpike House* features a cast that dates back to that decade: David Essex, who duets with Sarah on "Relocate", and the duo of Tony and Anthony Rivers, who sing all those eerie backing vocals. And for the most part, the characters who mill about on the album could be from any year in the second half of the twentieth century: a milkman, a barfly, a schoolgirl, a hostess, a couple considering a move to the countryside. I hesitate to use the word "timeless" but "retro" is out, so let's just say there's something classic here that rubs shoulders with the modern.

Tales from Turnpike House was one of the first albums I illegally downloaded in full, to make up for which I would eventually go on to buy four physical copies. I did, however, live in Leeds the first time I heard it, meaning most of the references in the lyrics went over my head. I had no idea, for example, what Goswell Road was, or where the 43 bus went, much less that the album title referred to a real building.

But London is often a necessary evil for a young journalist, and so by fate or coincidence, after seven years, two cities and six jobs, I ended up working at the *Islington Gazette*, which would have been your local newspaper if you'd actually lived in Turnpike House.

The *Gazette* isn't mentioned on *Turnpike*, thank god, but the album's first single "Side Streets" was inspired by the crime-obsessed *Croydon Advertiser*, which I suppose means a fictional (and I like to think unfairly maligned) version of my old paper is the source of the "bad press and horror stories" in the song.

Anyway, it turns out the 43 bus, Goswell Road, Turnpike House and the postcode EC1 are real things. If I wished, I could walk down the road right now and see them. But, weirdly, I still remember them the way I first knew them: as names that purely lived in Saint Etienne's music, so detached from my own life that they might as well have been made up or historical. I felt the same about Angel, London Fields, Tufnell Park, Haggerston, Mario's Cafe, Kentish Town, Primrose Hill, the mysterious and enticing jumble of places I'd only heard in the lyrics or titles of Etienne songs. So when I actually saw my first 43 bus in the wild, when I began working at the *Gazette*, cycling up Tufnell Park Road, drinking in London Fields, walking through Haggerston to get into town, what strange simultaneous blend of memory and discovery did I feel? I can't be the only one. Saint Etienne may be a London band beloved by Londoners, but they have plenty of fans who didn't know anything about the capital and populated the maps drawn in their discography with imagined streets and towers and parks and grime.

Long-time St Et collaborator and filmmaker Paul Kelly did live in Turnpike House in the early Noughties, but on the record Saint Etienne have filled in their own Fake 05 version of the building just like we filled in our own version of London. In fact, the Saints have established such a distance from the characters in these songs that Bob, Pete and Sarah are no longer in frame. The album cover shows only a cross-section of the building with its inhabitants making tea, doing yoga and watching TV. Turnpike House has been sliced open like a dolls' house and Saint Etienne are the gods peering in.

Front covers, like lyrics, often centre the music-makers — but in this case, we and the Saints are on the same side of the fourth wall. They are a film crew, visible only when they walk past a mirror. The *Foxbase Alpha* poster on one of the Turnpike House interior walls is one such object, a cheeky moment of self-reference, though they aren't actually pictured in that image either.

The fourth wall is so routinely broken in pop music as to be hardly there at all most of the time. Pop stars look into the camera, figuratively or literally, more often than not, even though of course they don't see us through the lens looking back. Saint Etienne are unusual because they rebuild this partition. The occasions when they write directly about themselves are the exception rather than the rule. They require a wall to be torn down where for most other bands there has only ever been a cavity.

Sex from a distance

If you actually did pull the side off a tower block and freeze time for long enough to make an album, one thing you might expect to see is some people with their clothes off.

Sex is, after all, the not-so-secret ingredient in pop music. Generally, you're meant to imagine against all the odds a direct relationship between the singer and yourself, to believe for the purposes of marketing that all those suggestive lyrics and smouldering looks into the camera are intended for your eyes and ears, or at least could be.

But all this depersonalisation — the way Saint Etienne separate themselves from their own work by being aloof, hard to understand, abstract, instrumental, French/not French, etc. — complicates things in this regard.

Saint Etienne are what happens in the spaces *around* sex. They pack lines into their songs like "in the bed where they make love", "the thrill hostess gave her first kiss", "like Demi Moore as she sighs", "the lipstick kiss, reminisce, awake till dawn". The sex is still there, but it isn't you who's having it. Sarah observes these scenes but she and her audience are outsiders, the bed and sighs and lipstick never Saint Etienne's or ours but belonging to the people at the centre of the action. Saint Etienne are the club, the camera, the corridor, the hotel room, the area beneath the pier.

Dance music and pop songs also have a logic and drive that is in itself kind of sexual, the way they build and release, so perhaps, in the case of songs like "He's on the Phone", there is a nameless subject moving through the sound-world of the record and having sex on its own terms, but it isn't either of the characters in the lyrics, who seem to be living lives beyond their own control. Nor is it Bob or Pete or Sarah. Maybe its experience is somehow reflected in the subconscious of the man on the phone or the woman holding her shoes, or in the pace and urgency with which we learn about them.

But certainly Saint Etienne will never look you in the face and seriously ask you to go to bed with them the way Jarvis Cocker or Janet Jackson or Shirley Manson or Paddy McAloon made careers out of doing so poetically and, well, fuckably. Even when Sarah admits "I know you want to hold my hand" on "Join Our Club", she goes on to insist that "you should call us up tonight" and you don't think for a second she means that it'll be just the two of you. And the St Et songs that look romantic on paper, "Nothing Can Stop Us" or "People Get Real" or "Hug My Soul", either seem impersonal to St Et themselves or are entirely unsexual in a way that partly reflects the chemical solipsism of acid house but perhaps more importantly reflects the fact Saint Etienne would be breaking the spell were they to be so literal and so mundane as to talk about lust.

Now I've mentioned control, it could be said that Saint Etienne achieve some of that distance by never quite allowing their characters the level of will that would typically be afforded to real people: there isn't a lot of motive in their songs and (insofar as one can determine what is going on in them at all) they often seem to describe a freezeframe rather than a narrative, like a flashbulb memory — which might explain why people rarely make decisions or see through processes in Etienne lyrics, why there is no "this town ain't big enough for both of us" or "don't marry her" or "kiss me" but mostly just rhetorical stuff like "he's so dark and moody/ she is his sunshine girl" and "he gave away all of her records/ is that where she belongs?" It would no more make sense for Sarah to proposition you on a St Et record than it would for Alfred Hitchcock to murder you in a shower scene.

Funnily enough, nowhere is the absent sex so noticeable as on "Shower Scene", the centrepiece of the *Finisterre* album, one of those great St Et should-have-beens that wasn't even released as a single in Britain. "Call my name," Sarah urges over and over in a manner that should be positively steamy.

But in this brave new world, a hot shower and a thunderstorm are indistinguishable.

If only we knew who was speaking, or to whom, maybe we could figure it all out, but the lyrics tell us nothing — "in the rain" one minute, "in the hall" the next, half-sentences with no subject, Sarah repeating (asking, pleading) "call my name" at the end of each verse. And of course calling someone's name could be sexual, but it could also mean they are lost. There is no *story* here, no agency, no "take me home" or "I want you". The truly seductive aspects of this song are the beat and the synthesisers and, yes, Sarah's voice in the abstract, but she's dissolved in the fog or the bath and now she haunts the track without form, waiting for someone to call her name, if she has one.

So far, so acid — those dance records without narrative, just snatches of "can you feel it?" and "take me higher" that could be love songs to the music itself[6] and seem to come from nowhere, certainly no one on stage or on the decks. But there's something sweeter and lonelier about "Shower Scene": it sounds like loss as well as liberation, uncertainty as well as unburdening.

Water. It sounds like water, far more than *Sound of Water*, the acoustic guitars that splash over the electronic pulse pushed way back in the mix, the fluid identities, the shower (in whatever context) washing away everything including the past

---

[6] Simon Reynolds makes the point about the reflexiveness of rave records — that lyrics that appear to be sexual could perhaps be better understood as love songs *about rave* — particularly well. See Simon Reynolds, "Rave Culture: Living Dream or Living Death?", in *The Clubcultures Reader*, ed. by Steve Redhead and others (Oxford: Blackwell, 1997), pp. 102-111 (pp. 104-107).

and the future and the I and the you leaving only a nameless now, and now this, and now this. Water can be cold abstract purity, or it can be movement, or drowning, or peaceful, or stagnant, always flowing but always *there*, caring little for the lives of people, impermanent or eternal, biding its time, slow but certain, rushing uncontrollably, in the Thames, in Tiger Bay, in the sea, in the showers, call my name.

Saint Etienne's distance from anything directly sexual is like a memory of sex, not *not sex* but also not sex here or now or with you, more like sex remembered at an entirely unsexual time when you recall more *that it happened* than how it actually felt.

Even the most direct first-person references to sex in Saint Etienne's records are alienated. They appear in cover versions — if not actually comic, then certainly absurd by being so out of place, just like the way they used to sprinkle bits of television into their albums: "I'm Too Sexy" by Right Said Fred, "Just Friends" by Amy Winehouse. Or they come in songs like "Your Valentine" with bizarre phrasing like "a kiss is imminent" and wrapped in a heavy somnambulant arrangement that sounds like a peaceful horror sequence, a solitary pair of headlights on a country road.

Another way of looking at it is that Saint Etienne's relationship with sex is pre-sexual, that it has more to do with the enduring lust for loveliness than it does lust for a person. It's the way we experience lust as children — that we are drawn to the things or even people that shine brightest in our universe but without the tedious business of sexual attraction, and therefore perhaps without the means to process or get over any of it. It's not that Sarah, as a singer, isn't seductive — she was the unparalleled indie girl pin-up for a generation of young adults. It's just that somewhere between all the sensual vocals and pumping basslines, no one actually gets off.

Maybe Sarah is the voice of memory, the woman digging through the filing cabinets in our head. The words Saint Etienne come out with exist where dreams and memories intersect. However logical or narrative they seem in the moment, they will always evaporate in the light of day. That explains how she can come so close without ever touching, a dream we're sure is real, a memory so vivid it feels like time travel until you come round.

Etienne gonna die. Whenever there's a risk of getting too involved with Sarah, she vanishes into an instrumental, a film, a change of perspective, another language, like a double agent, like a dream, like each of the Saints' albums is a collection of experiences after the fact, like someone remembering days and nights all pushed up against each other.

The macro version of DJ culture is treating whole records like samples, writing songs that jar with each other, using time, absenteeism, skits and the fourth wall to maintain a base level of estrangement that distances Saint Etienne as individuals from even their most straightforward material. But it also distances Saint Etienne from us, which is why we're observing them from all the way over here, and why it feels so transgressive to get near them.

Intermission

In the first part of this book, I've alleged that Saint Etienne set out to use and misuse memory like war artists firing off scrambled dispatches from the battle between now and then, reflections of and antidotes to the infinite recall and *fin de siècle* anxiety around them, the 1995-going-on-1965 (dis)comfort blanket of dumb nostalgia. Mainly, that meant Saint Etienne made albums that intentionally muddled up linear time through collage, catalogue and nonsense, and subsequently songs that falsely invoked the form and associations of memory for artistic effect. They did so partly as a rejection of the hierarchy of history, as a way to liberate the past from museums and put their own artefacts there instead. Sometimes this was a protest against authority, sometimes it was just funny, and sometimes it was about finding a stranger way of seeing the world, because Saint Etienne are almost religious about having no musical religion. I've also alleged that they did all this on a budget.

In the next part of this book, the Saints will turn the weapon of memory on themselves. They, and we, will retell our own stories as a means of understanding where we have ended up, which is to say more or less halfway through an argument, but also more or less halfway through the future.

do you remember where saint etienne used to live?

4.

London like a distant sun, London conversations, London is in your throat. Bob, Pete and Sarah grew up in towns that were defined by their relationship to the English capital: a magnetic pole, a humming presence with which commuters played chicken each day before returning tired or drunk to tell of (or lie about) their exploits. But the Saints didn't actually live *in* London until they were more or less grown up, grown up enough at least to use it how they wanted, by which time all its projected romance had soaked through them.

London never really washes out of Saint Etienne. But how they rationalise their memories of London, how they cope with its seduction and rejection, well, that's a matter of vantage point, time of day, time of life. And while they may at first have been having the time of their life, they knew increasingly that others had little time, or life, as towers and banks collapsed, developers got rich and inequality yawned.

Saint Etienne jammed references to London into their early records so that it was obvious the rail network connecting the Home Counties to the capital had been a neural system shuttling ideas about music and rebellion through their minds and souls as they grew up, and that the band's identity lay somewhere in that process. London jammed people into poor housing and public money into private pockets so that it was obvious the financial network connecting the City to the population that lived in the boroughs (and indeed the world) around it worked in only one direction, and that London's success lay somewhere in being able to obscure that fact.

But while that went on, London went on, inspiring bands and books and the kids on the outskirts in the way only it could. It was true that it had *more* of everything, and that sparks flew when more of everything came into contact with more of everything else — clubs, markets, squats, bars, warehouses, grooves, galleries, fashion, poppers, pills, pints, parks, £££. But it was also true that access to these things was limited, and that London's financial centre was one of the engines in a global machine that limited a lot of people's access to a lot of things.

Start again

Bob and Pete weren't long out of Croydon when they started writing about the capital city on whose extreme southern boundary they'd been born, young enough when they relocated to be taken in by its charm but old enough to understand something of how lucky they'd got — very slightly flush from their first record deal, dreaming in rented rooms, in the door, on the scene, just one turns into five turns into back to yours turns into the first bus home. At the time, it might have felt like London was on the cusp of something, just like they were. Ken Livingstone's Greater London Council had been gone since 1986, Thatcher having been unable to countenance a left-wing alternative power centre on her doorstep, but by 1990 the Iron Lady was on her way out too. The beginnings of gentrification were taking place, particularly in the former industrial Docklands, but the now-familiar hellscapes of half-empty luxury blocks anywhere there had once been pubs and music venues and good-quality social housing in zones 1 to 3 were still some way off.

And so *Foxbase Alpha* goes pretty easy on the capital, which had at some indiscernible point during the Seventies and Eighties also become *Saint Etienne's* capital. Of course it did: there was hardly anything to complain about. *Foxbase* was the opening salvo from three bright young music lovers who'd spent their childhoods orbiting London from safe suburban distances before touching down somewhere near Hampstead Heath. That much is evident from the hazy, carefree lyrics of "London Belongs to Me", and the psychogeographical essay on the back of the sleeve by Jon Savage, a romanticisation of precariousness as lifestyle: "Cash in your pocket puts a spring in your step. [...] The lowest point in the city — a sink for pollution, noise, destitution. But it's here that you find the raw material to make the world in the way that you hear it."

There are namechecks for Camden Town, Parkway, Primrose Hill and Tufnell Park, but the primary sense of London-ness comes simply from the fact it's a record of Saint Etienne having a kind of extended summer holiday there and assembling the sounds and feelings and places they came across into something that would have felt very familiar if you'd been there alongside them. *Foxbase Alpha* is in this sense little more than a scrapbook, precocious and at a pinch postmodern but still basically a diary.

Sarah: *Foxbase Alpha*, it's really got that London feel, I think, because all three of us, Bob, Pete and I, had all grown up in sort of the Home Counties — I was proper Home Counties, they were sort of Home Counties! — and had the same feeling like we just wanted to be in London and be a part of it. We'd grown up listening to the same kind of things and getting into the same kind of Sixties clothes, Fifties things, all that kind of stuff, going to see the same bands and everything. I think when *Foxbase Alpha* was made it was just like this massive melting pot. Although I wasn't involved in the songwriting on the record, I was very happy to be involved because it spoke to me, as it were. And all three of us were obsessed with London.

Pete: With *Foxbase Alpha* we were like kids. We'd just moved to London. We were having such a laugh generally — I'd given up a job to be in the band. It was like a dream, what was happening to us, but I suppose that's a bit inward and just thinking about yourself.

Saint Etienne recorded their follow-up, *So Tough*, in 1992, releasing it the following year. Tonally, it wasn't all that different from its predecessor but in its representation of London it possessed a level of realist detail not really apparent on *Foxbase*. You can hear it on a track like "Mario's Cafe" and in the field recordings of bars and cafes that spring up at different moments of the album. There was something slightly timeless about the glimpses of London on *Foxbase*; *So Tough* felt more in the action and of the moment.

By now in their late twenties, Saint Etienne must have known they were in the midst of something whose days were numbered — perhaps not Mario's Cafe itself,[1] which is in fact still operational at the time of writing, but certainly the group of people who meet there in the song's lyrics. The references loaded into "Mario's Cafe" (*Eubank wins the fight, and did you see the KLF last night?*) scribble down Saint Etienne's surroundings that year as though they are going out of fashion, which in a way they are because never again will they meet in quite the same way at the same table for the same conversations over the same newspapers and toast. "Mario's Cafe" and the tracks "Memo to Pricey" and "Chicken Soup" on *So Tough* form a scrappy triptych of the Saints' social lives, records and

---

[1] At any rate, despite the name, the song was actually inspired by the Moonlight Cafe on the western side of Brecknock Road, which is barely in Kentish Town at all.

recordings of two cafes and a bar, whose details would otherwise have been forgotten: things like the grain of Simon Price's voice as he talks, the Chanel ad that plays in the background, the contents of the *Racing Post*, if not the general recollection that these were places and people and things Saint Etienne knew well. Nor would anyone else have remembered in quite so much detail the scenes photographed in the CD booklet of kids coming home from school, smoking and laughing and hanging around phone boxes, probably not yet knowing they are making a record, if indeed they ever found out.

Once they'd got it on tape, 1992 ended. So did the love affair. There was a brief thematic relocation to Tiger Bay, then a European period that took them into the new millennium, and all told the Etienne weren't really back in London until a decade had passed.

The slightly revisionist title of their 2009 best-of *London Conversations* tried to obscure the fact that half their songs had nothing to do with London, but then maybe the conversations themselves had never stopped. Maybe Saint Etienne had never stopped reassessing their memories, their understanding of their place in London and what lay beyond its edges.

Tear it down

There is no permanent memorial to the four people who died when Ronan Point in east London collapsed in May 1968, nor any obvious sign in Butchers Road that the building was ever there.

A gas explosion on the eighteenth floor partially blew out one side of the tower, which hadn't been designed or built properly. Newham Council spent five years having the block patched up but it was still basically a fire trap when it reopened in 1973, in addition to which it leaked and swayed in the wind. The building was cleared out again in the mid-1980s and eventually demolished completely.

There is no permanent memorial to the four people who died when Ronan Point collapsed, save in a sense for the newsprint photo of its wreckage on the front cover of *Finisterre*, "*finis terrae*" being approximate Latin for "the end of the world", which is what it must have felt like for the people living there when the walls caved in.

The disaster triggered an inquiry and a string of new building regulations that were supposed to mark a turning point in the safety of high-rise and public housing. It turned out that several material factors had played a part in Ronan Point coming down, including its poor original design, various structural defects, the precise height of the explosion, and the faulty installation of the cooker whose leaking gas was lit up by an innocent match strike.

Most fundamentally, though, the catastrophe and its aftermath were political failures by Newham Council, first to ensure the quality of the build and then to listen to its residents. The tower wasn't condemned until 1984, and only then because of the persistence of the surviving occupants, twelve of whom had been injured in the original blast. That no further disasters happened there in the intervening period was more a matter of luck than anything else.

Yet much of the clamour resulting from the inquiry was performative and some of the work to make similar tower blocks safer was never even carried out.[2] Nor did the disaster

---

[2] Jules Birch, "Ronan Point 50 Years On: The Worrying Legacy of a Disaster", *Inside Housing* (May 14, 2018) <https://www.inside-housing.co.uk/comment/comment/ronan-point-50-years-on-the-

stop dangerous building and refurbishment work elsewhere from going ahead, even in the immediate proximity. Ronan Point fell down midway through the construction of the Broadwater Farm Estate a few miles away in Haringey, a project that used the same "large-panel system" that had been implicated in the collapse of Ronan Point — but work continued, even though the estate's homes, like Ronan Point, had gas supplies and would themselves have been at risk of collapse in the event of an explosion.[3]

Finisterre commemorated the end of the world in east London with a tombstone of destroyed kitchens. But it was also the end of the world in a political sense — it was the death of that first iteration of the band, of those three young music lovers who saw London as a playground.

As documentarists, the reborn Saint Etienne needed to confront not only the reality of the city they had once idolised but also the unreality of the records they had made about it. At times, *Finisterre* is like a retelling of *Foxbase Alpha*, a modernism that takes some of the ideas and structure from the Saints' debut to create something new. The roar of a football crowd at the start of the album? That's what you heard at the beginning of "This Is Radio Etienne". But the similarity only really serves to underline how different everything else is: songs like "Amateur", "Soft Like Me" and "The Way We Live Now" follow "Action" with nuanced storylines about

worrying-legacy-of-a-disaster-56236> [accessed September 26, 2021].

[3] Luke Barratt, "Broadwater Farm: A Large Panel System Case Study", *Inside Housing* (June 29, 2018) <https://www.insidehousing.co.uk/insight/insight/broadwater-farm-a-large-panel-system-case-study-57010> [accessed September 26, 2021].

hindsight, fairness and failure, responsibility and reckless-ness, lines like "this time I'm gonna say that we've gotta walk away", "rethink, refrain", "tear it down and start again", "we hold the key to the better way to be". Michael Jayston's BBC baritone slicing up rock and roll references like racing tips between tracks? You won't convince me that isn't a throwback to all the skits and samples sewn into Saint Etienne's debut. *Finisterre* was eclectic, just like *Foxbase* was a scrapbook of Bob, Pete and Sarah's favourite things. It's just that, by 2002, Saint Etienne were no longer only selecting the good bits from what they saw around them.

The road to hell is paved to the specifications of a municipal plan, following a public consultation

Finisterre was an area of sea in *The Shipping Forecast* until the year *Finisterre* was released, when it was unpopularly renamed FitzRoy. Broadcast on BBC Radio 4 in the middle of the night, *The Shipping Forecast* attracts a listenership that significantly outstrips the size of the actual maritime community that could conceivably find it useful. This is because it is comforting, both in its reliability (and thus its link to the past) and in its gentle, abstract escapism. It is a lamplit, come-as-you-are guided tour of the waters surrounding the British Isles, a series of peculiar, evocative proper nouns and a private grammar of distant gales and sleepy numbers lapping at the hull of an imaginary boat.

The sea names in *The Shipping Forecast* (Tyne, Forth, Cromarty, Forties, Malin and so on) also formed the basis for the lyrics of Blur's "This Is a Low" in 1994, whose huge-selling parent album *Parklife* was released a few weeks after *Tiger Bay*.[4] The song encapsulated both the soothing strangeness of the broadcast and Britpop's rose-tinted affection for the more esoteric corners of the BBC itself — a publicly funded national institution clinging on against a tidal wave of globalisation from the Atlantic. I bring this up because the rather manufactured idea so central to the Saints' Britpop contemporaries — that Britain had been any sort of utopian social democracy in the decades that followed the Second World War (*good, becoming moderate or poor later*) — is the opposite instinct of the one that created *Finisterre*, even though they share a suspicion of corporatised modernity.

Back on dry land, the Saints have more to say on the subject of the built environment. The memorial to destruction that adorns *Finisterre*'s front cover is one pillar of its representation of urban life (and death), but the record is capacious, or unsteady, enough for a second that is more concerned with its erosion than with the moment of its precipitous collapse into the streets of Newham.

That pillar is the language and imagery of municipal planning — particularly planning as a means to influence behaviour and attitudes, and implicitly the belief that it is possible to simply design one's way out of a social problem. (The two themes are related, of course, because Ronan Point

---

[4] Blur and Saint Etienne always seemed to have a new album out around the same time as each other between 1991 and 1994. The only year in which the Saints outsold Blur was 1993; *Parklife* rocketed Damon Albarn and co. to megastardom the following spring, while Saint Etienne fell out of the top ten with *Tiger Bay* almost immediately, never to return.

had to pass through municipal planning, housing and building regulations departments before it fell down.)

Saint Etienne's interest in this subject also has its roots in Bob and Pete's upbringing in Croydon. The town's post-war concrete reconstruction was booming by the Sixties and Seventies in the form of modern office blocks and major transport projects that reflected, and in some cases competed with, central London's own growth ten or so miles to the north.

And so, on the reverse of the wreckage of Ronan Point, in the Impact typeface of a newspaper bill poster, these words are printed on the back of the album cover:

HAVE THERE BEEN ANY ATTEMPTS, THROUGH PLANNING, TO EITHER DISCOURAGE OR PROMOTE CERTAIN PATTERNS OF BEHAVIOUR IN YOUR NEIGHBOURHOOD? (WHICH/HOW?)

Another display inside reads:

STRATEGIES OF SOCIAL CLOSURE IN URBAN AND REGIONAL PLANNING.

The projects from which these words were cut out by Danish collage artist Jakob Kolding are not identified. But the strategies their authors likely had in mind may well have ended up in the landmark 2004 UK government document *Safer Places: The Planning System and Crime Prevention*, which drew together nearly a decade of New Labour thinking about how to be seen to deal with crime without mentioning inequality or capitalism.

There is, therefore, no effort to address poverty in *Safer Places*, nor any obvious sign in its pages that the problem exists at all. It does, however, make reference to "rowdy youths", "disorderly people" and those with a "general predisposition to offend".

None of this is particularly surprising from a Labour Party whose leader thought the left "did not take sufficiently seriously the belief in personal responsibility" when it talked about crime.[5] Unfortunately, while chasing middle-class voters by fussing about things like how to stop kids hanging around in groups, Labour had largely turned a blind eye to the real crime that the planning system could have been marshalled to help solve: the unavailability of affordable homes, even though providing people with a safe and stable home has been recognised as a solution to so many other social problems (such as health inequality, addiction and unemployment, as well as crime).[6]

When Labour came to power in 1997, there were a little over a million households (1.02m) on waiting lists for housing in England.[7] That figure had grown to 1.74m when the party

[5] "Interview with Tony Blair", *On the Record*, BBC Two, July 4, 1993 <http://www.bbc.co.uk/otr/intext92-93/Blair4.7.93.html> [accessed July 23, 2021].

[6] See, for instance, Alex S Vitale on the comparative costs of providing housing and repeatedly dragging people through the criminal justice system, in *The End of Policing* (London: Verso, 2017), p. 97. Vitale's data refers to the US, but UK councils such as Hackney in north London have, in recent years, begun trialling the internationally successful "Housing First" programme of inter- vention, which gives people a home before trying to get them to engage with other services.

[7] Ministry of Housing, Communities and Local Government, "Households on Local Authority Waiting List" dataset (2020)

left office in 2010. But the number of social homes that were actually available was going down: 84,102 were sold under right-to-buy in 2003/4, the peak during the Labour years, compared with just 22,661 new ones completed.[8]

Labour in fact spent even less on social housing in its first term than the Tories had during their final years in power.[9] When spending did at last begin to increase, the year *Finisterre* came out,[10] it was desperately inadequate to reverse the attrition of council housing, partly because much of it went on the (necessary) work of improving the standards of existing ones and partly because of rising land prices.[11] The 2004 Barker Review called for a much larger investment into social housing to stabilise the amount of available stock, but this

---

<https://data.london.gov.uk/dataset/households-local-authority-waiting-list-borough> [accessed September 28, 2021].

[8] Ministry of Housing, Communities and Local Government, table 678 ("Annual Social Housing Sales by Scheme for England") (2020) <https://www.gov.uk/government/statistical-data-sets/live-tables-on-social-housing-sales> [accessed September 28, 2021] and table 1000 ("Additional Affordable Homes Provided by Type of Scheme, England") (2020) <https://www.gov.uk/government/statistical-data-sets/live-tables-on-affordable-housing-supply> [accessed September 28, 2021].

[9] Gene Robertson, "Labour's Legacy", *Inside Housing* (May 7, 2010) <https://www.insidehousing.co.uk/insight/insight/labours-legacy-19459> [accessed September 27, 2021].

[10] Kate Barker, *Review of Housing Supply Final Report — Recommendations*, paragraph 34 (London: HMSO, 2004) <http://news.bbc.co.uk/nol/shared/bsp/hi/pdfs/17_03_04_barker_review.pdf> [accessed September 28, 2021].

[11] Ibid.

took three further years to happen, by which time Labour had been in power for a decade: the government didn't manage to get more social homes built than were being lost through right-to-buy and other sales until 2007.[12]

Strangely enough, despite both main parties' ideological obsession with individual responsibility, no one seemed to want to take individual responsibility for the way governments of both colours had contributed to the housing crisis by enabling and incentivising the conversion of public housing into private profit — nor for the building of unaffordable private homes as "investment opportunities" while poorer families languished on waiting lists, crammed into inadequate temporary accommodation that limited their life chances, their ability to work, and their children's ability to study and even learn to walk.

There is no effort to address poverty in *Safer Places*, save in a sense for the sole example of "lack of leisure facilities" as the kind of "wider life circumstance" that might motivate people to offend. *Safer Places* is more about moving problems — poverty, deprivation, inequality — than fixing them.

You and I were made complicit in this doublethink through the now-familiar mechanisms of illusory democracy. While in power, first the Tories and then Labour insisted that local councils should increase the amount of public consultation

[12] Compare table 678 ("Annual Social Housing Sales by Scheme for England") <https://www.gov.uk/government/statistical-data-sets/live-tables-on-social-housing-sales> [accessed September 28, 2021] with table 1000 ("Additional Affordable Homes Provided by Type of Scheme"), England <https://www.gov.uk/government/statistical-data-sets/live-tables-on-affordable-housing-supply> [accessed September 28, 2021].

they were doing — partly, it has been suggested, as a trick to appease traditional Conservative bases (including those that voted Labour in 1997) whose objection to development was a growing problem for governments that wanted to court big business (if not, particularly, to build affordable homes).[13]

The bold, pseudo-friendly questions about crime and planning plastered over *Finisterre*'s artwork may therefore have come from the mandatory consultations that every town hall was required by the 2000 Local Government Act to carry out as part of setting a "community strategy". These strategies were plans for how each council would "promot[e] or improv[e] the economic, social and environmental well-being of their area and contribut[e] to the achievement of sustainable development in the United Kingdom".[14]

---

[13] The Tories' "local choice" agenda, for instance, increased the importance of development plans set in each area to help councils make planning decisions, and thus "gave the impression of devolution of control to localities in resolving decision-making" (Philip Allmendinger and Mark Tewdwr-Jones, "New Labour, New Planning? The Trajectory of Planning in Blair's Britain", *Urban Studies*, vol. 37, no. 8 (2000), pp. 1379-1402 (p. 1384) <www.jstor.org/stable/43196559> [accessed July 18, 2021]) — yet simultaneously told councils what they could actually put in those development plans, and thus what sorts of planning applications would get approved or declined. According to Allmendinger and Tewdwr-Jones, rather than increasing accountability or public control of services, all this really did was make local councils into a shield for problems created by the national government.

[14] UK Government, Local Government Act 2000, section 4 <https://www.legislation.gov.uk/ukpga/2000/22/enacted> [accessed July 27, 2021].

The anticipated answers would surely have been the sorts of strategies recommended in *Safer Spaces*. But clear-eyed local authorities did not need community strategies to understand that their "economic and social well-being" was imperilled by the fact they were unable to adequately house thousands of their most vulnerable people.[15]

While it mandated councils to go out and speak to the great unwashed about what on earth their neighbourhoods could possibly need, Labour's failure at a national level to stabilise the loss of affordable homes for the most part kicked the problem downhill to those same town halls.[16] Meanwhile, one of the government's solutions to the £19bn council housing repair bill it had inherited was the mass offloading of the units' management and ownership onto unelected housing associations, and — to put it politely — it is hard to see how this could have increased accountability for anyone.

---

[15] Gene Robertson, "Labour's Legacy", *Inside Housing* (May 7, 2010) <https://www.insidehousing.co.uk/insight/insight/labours-legacy-19459> [accessed September 28, 2021].

[16] The closest Islington came in its own community strategy to anything about increasing housing supply was the unhelpfully vague commitment to "ensure that a proportion of new housing units remain genuinely affordable and available to those on an intermediate salary". See London Borough of Islington, *Sustainable Community Strategy* (London: London Borough of Islington, 2007), p. 13 <https://democracy.islington.gov.uk/Data/Council/200712041930/Agenda/SCS%20Draft%20Strategy.pdf> [accessed July 27, 2021]) By the time I joined the *Gazette* in 2016, the housing waiting list was roughly equal to the number of units sold through right-to-buy since 1980.

Hope and power

The first examples I can remember of the drive to "design out" places for vulnerable people were those shit bus stop benches that were installed at an angle so unaccommodating they were almost impossible to sit on, much less sleep on. But people got a lot more creative than that in their efforts to be cruel. There were also

> spiked window-sills, 45° "decorative" railings, concrete wedges, studded flower-planters and automatic sprinkler systems which come on in the middle of the night to "clean" shop and office doorways [that] are being used to repel the public from the edge of the street.[17]

Still, by 2002, the kids had not been fully repelled. One image in the *Finisterre* CD booklet overlaid with the words ARCHITECTURAL BOUNDARIES AND SPATIAL FLOWS: STRATEGIES FOR REGULATION like a ransom note shows them skateboarding beneath a flyover, a blank zone within the road network, a place fleetingly hidden from the bird's eye by the motorway that covers it, the London nobody knows, not unlike the black-and-white photos of laughing schoolchildren in the *So Tough* artwork. They pick their way through car parks in the lyrics of *Finisterre*'s title track, finding "new spaces, new routes, new areas". They'll never be able to afford houses in their own

---

[17] Iain Borden, "Thick Edges: Architectural Boundaries in the Postmodern Metropolis", in *InterSections: Architectural History and Critical Theory*, ed. by Iain Borden and Jane Rendell (London: Routledge, 2001), pp. 221-246 (pp. 225-226).

city. But there is a DIY optimism in their very presence, in *Finisterre* as a whole, in the new millennium and new mayor, that the entropy of youth is some sort of permanent resistance against the commodification and delimitation of the city, not unlike the way illegal samples and illegal parties were acts of resistance against prescriptive public order and copyright laws in the days of *Foxbase Alpha*.[18]

Pete: The new towns, when they were made, they were quite good, but they're just not maintained properly and so they become the opposite of what they were meant to be. We kind of like municipal behaviour and projects that could enrich everybody's lives, but they often don't turn out that easy or they're short-lived. The old graphics for a lot of those things appeals to us because we grew up in Croydon, me and Bob, and it was all very concrete-y and I initially hated it and then grew to really like all that, imagining it was a bit like *Captain Scarlet*, a sort of future vision for everybody. But it tends to go wrong and it's not as rosy as the pictures, as it's presented. There's some good intentions and then cycles of different governments coming in and out and then different projects failing and some hope and promise and then it sort of fades away.

The contradiction on this album, in its songs and its artwork, is about power: between the call to "tear it down and start again" in the chorus of "Finisterre" and the recurring theme of people having things done to them — the

---

[18] Most notoriously, the Criminal Justice and Public Order Act 1994, the law that clumsily attempted to stop outdoor parties by proscribing music with "repetitive beats".

communities scattered across outer London in the post-war period, the council tenants whose homes blew up, the characters in "Amateur" who "become very ill" because of a phone mast, the "rowdy youths" and "disorderly people" who are being "designed out" of their own neighbourhoods. It's a tension between adversity and optimism. *Finisterre* is, after all, the record of a juncture in British history — the Nineties and Noughties colliding; a period when you could make digital films of people using paper tickets on the Tube; a young Labour government poised to tip into militarised neoliberal extremism.

Pete: There was an idea to find out what London meant to people in a frank way. We were still writing about the magic or the appeal of London, or why people were drawn to it, but I guess it was probably a bit more other people's experiences rather than ours.

Sarah: I grew up in Windsor — as soon as I could go to London I did. It was so magnetic and you just felt like there was something going on. I've always had this feeling that London is pretty much the best city in the world. If I go for too long without going, I feel like I'm missing something.

It was clothes and it was gigs. My friend and I, my best friend from school, we used to get on the train and go up to Kensington Market and King's Road and sometimes buy some really ill-thought-out Adam Ant type jacket or something. That's why we went.

For most of my teenage years, I used to visit London every time I had a birthday, spending my saved-up Sunday wages and record tokens at Sister Ray and Reckless and any of the seemingly hundreds of branches of the Music & Video Exchange. Because my birthday is in April, the city I saw was always in a state of new life, the parks and streets busy with tourists and skateboarders and boomboxes and blossom. The metal Tube stations and Big Bang architecture were nothing like the buildings I was used to, and there were records in the shops that you simply couldn't get in Bristol, where vinyl hardly seemed to exist any more. This started the same year that *Finisterre* came out and I can see that naive millennial excitement in the album, too, in Kolding's collages of DJs and music equipment, workers and buildings, on the back and the inside. It's the other vibe. It's why the sun and the darkness share the space above what was then London's skyline.

Look up/look back

You're never more than six feet from a tower block.[19] This transatlantic icon of late-twentieth-century housing and work is frequently pictured on Saint Etienne's album and single covers because it is always visible beneath the clouds, its glassy surfaces a mirror to the sky, its concrete surfaces a mirror to the ground.

What's almost revolutionary is that Saint Etienne allow towers to look good. At one end of the spectrum, there's Turnpike House looking smart and welcoming on *Tales from Turnpike House*, despite the conservative narrative about inner-city tower blocks being unkempt antisocial behaviour magnets. At the other, there's Brazil's bicameral National Congress building looking majestic and otherworldly on *Built*

---

[19] This isn't true.

on Sand, despite the destructive right-wing governments it has housed.

Then there are the thrilling glimpses drawn or photographed for record covers like *Travel Edition*, *I Love to Paint* and *Foxbase Beta*, silhouettes, walls, windows and reflections. Even putting Ronan Point on the front of *Finisterre* is more a criticism of recklessness, of white-collar negligence, than any judgement of the architecture itself — a reversal of the logic that produced *Safer Spaces*, namely that crime can be blamed on the design of people's homes instead of economics.

Saint Etienne would continue to resist the revisionist stereotype, partly set in motion by Ronan Point itself, that high-rises necessarily represent trouble or deprivation[20] — *Tales from Turnpike House*, which came three years after *Finisterre*, was one of pop music's most sympathetic portraits of a tower block since the Bee Gees' love-letter to Kilburn Towers in the late Sixties. The skyscrapers of the rich, offices and penthouses are nodes of unearned power and wealth that are bought and sold while cash-strapped councils struggle to maintain the high-rises where people actually live. But some of London's best-quality council housing was built in towers too, a great deal of it now lost to the private sector.

Separately from all that is the way they look, like the future in the air: skyscrapers, done right, can take your breath away with their sublime scale and their dizzying *up*, and it's OK to remember when you see them the belief that London belonged to you even when it didn't, to remember that even

---

[20] Peter Hall, *Cities of Tomorrow: An Intellectual History of Urban Planning and Design Since 1880*, fourth edition (Chichester: Wiley-Blackwell, 2004), pp. 271-272.

monuments to capitalism stirred feelings that couldn't exactly be given words.

But they could be given pictures, and so skyscrapers play a leading role in the feature film that accompanied *Finisterre*. It was around this time that the band, suddenly discovering their visual work didn't need to be constrained to record covers, began taking their role as archivists more seriously. *Finisterre* was a feature-length portrait of London's metamorphosis and self-cannibalism, a day in the city with its artists and musicians, all at various stages of leaving and arriving, approaching its many faces and all its hope and disappointment in more detail and thus with more nuance than they'd typically done on record. It was like they realised London wasn't going to wait around for them to change their minds again.

In a different sense, this wasn't all that new, because what are documentaries if not collages? The *Finisterre* film is a patchwork of samples, not unlike *Foxbase Alpha* or *So Tough*, except that these samples are visual as well as aural, found sights as well as found sounds. Now you can press the rattle of a train up against the shape of an office block, "Shower Scene" up against footage of a storm in the city. You're welcome. In a way, it's surprising it took the Etienne so long to start making documentaries given the obvious similarities to the way they had first worked on audio tape, not to mention the fact everyone had been saying their songs sounded like movies from the word go.

Or maybe the music and the films had some common ancestry. *Finisterre* (the film) took its cue from *The London Nobody Knows*, the book (by Geoffrey Fletcher) and subsequently film (by Norman Cohen) that stitched together a picture of the capital not from its glamour but from its grime, its streets, its performers, its houses and ghettos, its everyday life, its dereliction, its dialects and diets, its people, and crucially from the parts of it that were on the way out: slums, survivors of war, a pie shop, a boarded-up music hall. The signifiers had changed by 2002, most of them, but when Saint Etienne, Paul Kelly and Kieran Evans came to film *Finisterre* they looked for the same disappearances to tell a story about their unbreakable but troublesome connection to the capital.

Bob: *The London Nobody Knows* was made in '67 and went to places like Chapel Market and Bankside when they were really off the beaten track — obviously London was still just about swinging in '67 and the bits of it you saw on film would always have been Carnaby Street and maybe Soho but certainly not Islington, which was still part of the East End then. So we'd always wondered, if you had the opportunity, what bits of London would you film now in the same way that the James Mason film recorded bits of disappearing London?

When we did *Finisterre* we went to Beggars Banquet with the idea of making a full-length film, or basically a video for each song on the album, which would then be a separate DVD, and they gave us some money to do the first couple of singles and then got cold feet, so we ended up making the whole film for the budget of two singles. No one got rich out of it. But it worked out alright. We were really happy with it.

There were things like cafes that had been there since the Fifties. It was very obvious they were going because people were retiring and their kids either weren't interested in keeping the business on or rents were going up so much they were being squeezed out. It's amazing how many cranes you see in *Finisterre*. And then bits of post-war office stock that are now gone. There's a really bizarre set of concrete struts that were in mid-air above a petrol station on Clerkenwell Road — right behind where the *Frieze* [magazine] office was — and they were demolished within weeks of us filming them. And they were very hard to demolish because they were made of solid concrete, so I remember going to the *Frieze* office and it was incredibly noisy for weeks.

The London Nobody Knows was a touchstone for me and Paul [Kelly], which we just both remembered from being on ITV on afternoons in the Eighties when you were on the dole and you would end up seeing these random things.[21]

The London Nobody Knows makes for confrontational viewing in the twenty-first century: James Mason seems rueful as he tours the Sixties city, like he blames the people who watch documentaries for the worst of the changing world and of what came before it. He has a point, prescient though it may have been — the aestheticisation of working-class spaces by middle-class people has undoubtedly helped both drive and whitewash their gentrification and destruction.

Which in a way brings us back to *Foxbase Alpha* and the Saints' own romanticisation of north London in the early Nineties through the lenses of music and markets and life on

---

[21] The tornado of reference and memory swirling around Saint Etienne probably owes a lot to those afternoons: during this period Bob may well also have encountered or re-encountered *Tiger Bay*, the 1959 film, *The Way We Live Now*, the 1875 novel or the 1969 dramatisation, *How We Used to Live*, the educational series that aired from the late Sixties until the beginning of this century, or the Norman Collins novel *London Belongs to Me*, all of which had their titles repurposed as songs or albums sooner or later.

the dole while you tried to make it as a pop star. These instincts weren't entirely middle-class, and nor were Saint Etienne as people, but there is something very middle-class about Saint Etienne as a concept — the essence of their early career in particular was aspirational, stylish, out of reach, which isn't a criticism, because distance is thrilling, but nor is it a political endorsement. *Finisterre* is a reappraisal of all this, of London as a real place where real people live and die, and maybe that explains why they made a film about the bits of London that were vanishing out of the grasp of ordinary people at the same time as they made an album that seemed to recall and revisit their first.

But of course the process of change and memory carried on after *Finisterre* had been and gone. Saint Etienne, who didn't see *The London Nobody Knows* until it was twenty years old, must have similarly expected a proportion of their own viewers to be watching after the fact too, experiencing the films as time capsules, and thus to have been faced with some awkward truths of their own. Many of the nascent changes documented in Saint Etienne's film work over the years — the Lower Lea Valley before the 2012 Olympic bid built over it (*What Have You Done Today, Mervyn Day?*), the fortunes of greasy spoons (*Today's Special*), the redevelopment of the South Bank (*This Is Tomorrow*), land grabs, demolition, rejuvenation — had grown to giant proportions by the time of the Saints' first film festival, in 2021 at the BFI, and would have forced members of the audience to question or admit their own role in those changes.

Sarah: The thing about London is it does change, and part of you goes: "Oh no, don't change." I embrace change if it's for the good. Sometimes it's not. Like we did that film

[*Today's Special*] about cafes, where they just kept getting closed down all the time, and that is really sad. But I guess cities have to evolve, don't they? They can't just stay exactly the same.

Where I live, there's a lot of beautiful green spaces that are being threatened with development. If it were to happen, I would feel like archiving the beautiful stuff around here before it's taken away. You don't want people to forget it or not to have known it.

It's about sharing stuff that other people who've never been to London or lived around it haven't experienced — that this is what it's like. It may change soon but it's important to share stuff. I think Saint Etienne has always been a very sharing band. I remember when we put "Join Our Club" out, all these people going, "so elitist, Saint Etienne, 'our club'," and we're going: "No, no!" Saint Etienne is all about going, "listen to this brilliant music," "here's this brilliant sample," "listen to this, it's great," or "watch this".

This love of sharing is one thing that hasn't really changed as Saint Etienne have developed as people and artists and Londoners, because a commons (even a commons of sound) is the opposite of gentrification. Gentrification is the colonisation of the commons, the imposition of boundaries both physical and financial by those with the most privilege around what had been the property of everyone: public housing, public space. And so on a couple of levels, Saint Etienne had been railing against gentrification even when they were aestheticising the inner city, and it was inevitable that they would eventually progress to filmmaking the moment Jacques Vendroux began talking in "This Is Radio Etienne". Now they can share sights and stories as well as sounds, like a library of London.

File under fiction

Saint Etienne had been making films for nearly twenty years by the time of their 2021 project *I've Been Trying to Tell You*. Like *Finisterre*, *I've Been Trying to Tell You* was a multimedia affair, a record and a film that were equal partners. Though Saint Etienne had been prolific in the arenas of both music and film during those two decades, *I've Been Trying to Tell You* was a new proposition: it contained actors and had something resembling a storyline. Previously, the closest they'd come to this was *What Have You Done Today, Mervyn Day?*, their 2005 film about the Lower Lea Valley, but even then the character of Mervyn the paperboy really only functioned as an on-screen narrator, the glue holding together the factual segments of the documentary. There's nothing to narrate in *I've Been Trying to Tell You*.

The film looks and sounds like the fever dream of someone poorly remembering youth in old age. It's the memory of a view of the world that Saint Etienne had all but discarded years earlier through *Finisterre*. It's the choice of nostalgia over history to prove a point.

Sarah: It's about misremembering things. You remember the good bit, or you imagine it was all really good at that point in time, and then you start scrutinising it and going: "Yeah, but was it?"

There's a lot of youth involved, especially in the film, a lot of — what it was like to be young and carefree and stuff, but also to believe in things and then realise that maybe you shouldn't have believed in them. It's quite a vague idea that I think all three of us interpreted slightly differently.

This is what I've been trying to tell you and what they've been trying to tell us the whole time. Unreliable is exactly what the memories of London are on *Foxbase Alpha* and *So Tough* because on one hand it isn't really London that has changed but the Saints, and on the other hand we all know London *has* changed since the Nineties, but who can prove it? Maybe the gentrification was less advanced. Maybe there were more pockets of resistance. Maybe those pockets were only tolerated because they stopped people focusing on what was wrong.

I've Been Trying to Tell You, the album and the film, is the unreliable memory brought to half-life, slo-mo shots of young people with flawless skin running through the sunshine, swimming in open water, skimming stones, dancing and fucking and quoting the lyrics of songs released before they were born, a break or a bassline or a vocal rising out of the mist without anything to anchor it like the bar you sing to yourself over and over trying to work out where it's from or what comes next. It's about the real memory of a Fake 97 (the samples in the music are primarily taken from songs released between 1997 and 2001). It's the first St Et feature film that doesn't concern itself with capturing *what is* and instead takes us back to a hazy world that never existed, but which all of us remember regardless of what year we lived through it. I remember it. I remember being outside on hot nights, writing songs, burning CDs, drinking until I was sick. And, above all, boys. And, above boys, records.

For all these reasons, *I've Been Trying to Tell You* feels like one of those left-turns for Saint Etienne. But it seems a whole lot less surprising if you take a look at what the Saints had been doing in the years leading up to it.

Since 2017, Bob and Pete (and occasionally Sarah) have curated a large and growing range of primarily Sixties and Seventies compilation albums for the British reissue label Ace Records. They are, essentially, playlists around a non-musical theme, imaginary soundtracks, meditations expressed using existing songs. The subject matter could be a particular point in European or American history and its attendant politics and national mood, or a portrait of a city, or even the comings and goings at a particular bar. They have evocative but open-ended titles like *Three-Day Week* or *English Weather* or *Occasional Rain*.

This might seem a bit inconsistent with everything I've argued so far, which is that Saint Etienne are meticulously modern and never dwell for too long on the past without shaping it into something new. What's more, Bob and Pete were only born halfway through the Sixties and even their memories of the Seventies would have been distorted and intensified by youth. Nor did they experience any of the set pieces that crop up on these albums, things like visiting Kreuzberg with Iggy Pop or touring America in the wake of Vietnam. Their credentials as mixtapers, and as lovers of the music made in the Sixties and Seventies, aren't in question, but they've never made records *about* the past before.

But these compilation albums aren't about yearning for the remembered past to return; they're about the creative act of assembling a past that fits the distorted memory. They give form to all those Fakes wound up on the cassettes in Bob and Pete's minds. I could do something similar for my Fake 95, we all could, for the high-gloss desperation that songs from that year sound like to me, but it would be a different playlist from what you might put together to represent that year. The past is subjective.

Pete: It's not a definitive take on "this is the best of post-punk" or "the best of Seventies junk shop glam". It's more, within the sort of idea that we've come up with, this is *our* take.

I think there's an element of romanticising, but there's also an element of seeing the grime and the differences in the way it was in Britain, actually thinking a bit more about the period and what it was like to live then — and the restrictions people had on recording and the amount of money, and gloomy politics and things going on in the world. The bit we find romantic is the music that came from people's responses to what was going on in the world, rather than thinking everything was great in those days.

Maybe we used to be like that a bit when we did *Foxbase Alpha*, like "the Sixties was great" and all that, and as you get a bit older you're a bit more, actually, things have always been shit to varying degrees in daily life for a lot of people. Again, in our aesthetic — and it's something that's shared by people like Earl Brutus and World of Twist and the Fall — is a sort of celebration of the slightly naff bits. There's a kind of Britishness that's a bit naff. That goes with a lot of the Seventies and Sixties music and some of the imagery — like the cover of *English Weather* — there's something — I don't know if it's noble, but there's something that we like about the slightly crap-ness of Britain.

Bob: On *Three-Day Week*, we really wanted to make a compilation that sounded like you could hear the power cuts and the strikes. Records that suggested studio time was rationed and musical instruments were rationed. There was thinner vinyl because of the oil shortages. It's such a peculiar period in British history.

I'm really interested in social history and I think it can be written in so many different ways, and especially having lived through the Nineties and seen how that gets written up now — it's fascinating because a lot of it's not how I remember it.

It's not like we're right and other people are wrong, not at all, but that's how we remember or how we see it. With *English Weather*, I have very vague memories of that period 'cause I was five years old, but I can remember how it felt — seeing people sat on Box Hill with guitars, like hippies and bikers, and this kind of feeling, even at the time, that people were mourning the fact the Sixties had ended and didn't really know what the Seventies were going to be, which lasted until glam really — it's a really odd time. I was kind of dimly aware of that even as a child, and so finding a soundtrack to that feeling — it felt like we were onto something there and it wasn't just some weird notion in our heads. It was something that was intangible but we could make it more real by putting these compilations together.

Bob and Pete tried again and again with their Ace Records albums to get at these mental pictures: clouds on the moors (*Tim Peaks*), Paris in the spring (*Paris in the Spring*), LA in the afternoon (*Songs for the Fountain Coffee Room*), soul in the synthesiser (*The Tears of Technology*). English weather, English ghosts, French films, German bars, American records. Trains of thought from Victoria to coastal towns, stuck in the past behind who knows what. Running out of vinyl and running out of the city.

St Et hadn't made an album that bowed under the weight of all the old records and films cut into it since *So Tough* in 1993. So it's easy to see how the Ace collections might have been a subconscious influence on the Saints' decision to return to samples during lockdown with *I've Been Trying to Tell You* — and, more fundamentally, to turn (back) to imagined memory.

Not that the songs on the Ace Records albums can really be called samples. All of them feature in full. They're labelled and contextualised with sleevenotes, nothing like the unidentified snaps of noise and dialogue and rhythm on *Foxbase* and *So Tough*. The Ace Records albums aren't Saint Etienne albums. But just like the songs they cut up for *I've Been Trying to Tell You*, the goal in bringing them together is to give a name to something nameless, to agree feelings and ideas rather than facts and dates. Maybe Saint Etienne have always been making the case for feelings and ideas, desperately trying to share the products of that fluid space between mood and memory just to prove they aren't mad.

Bob: I think all the films we've made are trying to capture something that maybe wouldn't be captured otherwise. If nobody else has done it, then we should probably film it or put a compilation together ourselves, or make sense of it ourselves and write a script or an essay to accompany that and make it relatable to other people. It's nothing to do with nostalgia. It's more about social history. I don't like nostalgia. There's bound to be a melancholy that comes out of looking back on a period where you can't really touch it any more, but it's not nostalgia. I wouldn't really want to live through the mid-Seventies again — it wasn't really any better than the place we're in now.

While Saint Etienne were making *Foxbase Alpha*, I don't think it occurred to any of them that 1991 might not be as good as it got, or that there was anything about London that they didn't know. By the time they got to *Foxbase Beta* eighteen years later, it seemed the real question was how much better the record could have been had it only not been made in 1991 at all.

It isn't that the Saints don't still miss London when they stay away too long. Nor is it that they don't still miss the parts of London that have been driven out in the name of wealth and globalisation. But *Finisterre* was the moment the penny dropped that there are no neutral observers. It's the sight and sound of a band recalibrating.

That's why *Tales from Turnpike House* is a collection of fiction-alised perspectives about the capital. It's why *How We Used to Live* is a subversive re-edit of other people's footage. When Saint Etienne look back now, on the Ace albums or *I've Been Trying to Tell You*, they understand that memory is often wrong, and that you can't remember what you didn't understand in the first place. It's a lesson they've learnt the hard way, which is also the best way. Yes, maybe that's the point.

do i remember how i used saint etienne to live?

5.

The members of Saint Etienne had childhoods that were sponsored by the British Phonographic Industry, the kind where music came first and everything else a distant second. You can recognise people who grew up like this because of the slightly strange way they talk about the world twenty or thirty or forty years later, which makes sense if you understand that it abstractly reproduces the logic of certain non-abstract rules and processes — the league table of the singles chart, the understanding of what a side one track one should sound like, the compilation albums, the pocket money, the scraps of paper you brought to second-hand shops, an A-Z of the nearest metropolitan centre, the back issues of *Record Collector*, and the discs and tapes inching their way slowly along the margins of the floor in search of a proper storage unit. Often these people support third-division football clubs and get through a lot of notebooks. Top trumps, first pressing, second pressing, all out for forty-five. Picture sleeve. Writing on label. Very good to very good plus, becoming moderate later.

Maybe there is a recognition of kindred spirits when you encounter a band like Saint Etienne, whose music seems so clearly shaped by those same values, learnt by rote while perched in front of the radio writing down the top forty. Maybe Saint Etienne attract people who had the same kind of childhood, like a subsonic signal buried in their records saying: I bet you can tell me all the British Christmas number ones between 1985 and 1999 without looking them up. Think about it — the albums made like mixtapes, the highly detailed selective memories that always involve music, the unspoken logic of their decisions and all the links and references you'd only know if you'd learnt them the long way, the cataloguing and re-cataloguing of their own past, the iconography you could doodle in an exercise book, the reconstruction of ritual because they needed us to experience their music the way they had experienced T-Rex, the Bee Gees, the Beach Boys, the Monkees or whoever, the collective understanding that every Saint Etienne record to date is an important piece of context for whatever they make next just like every experience in your life is an important piece of context for whatever you experience next.

The story of my relationship with Saint Etienne, and I would wager the story of yours, is a story about lists, about words and music as units of measurement, just like the story of their relationship with memory is a story about lists, or perhaps just subsets of one universal list, the tracklist for the tape that is always recording.

Some people collect setlists. My best friend used to keep a list of all the bands he had seen. But Saint Etienne are a group whose essence is on record, whose soul is in the studio. They are a band of minute adjustments, ghosts in the machine, devils in the detail. So the list that tells the real story of my relationship with the Saints is the inventory of all the Saint Etienne records I bought and was bought and borrowed and gave away over the years, and should such an inventory exist it would begin here, with what we might as well call item one, *Smash Hits 1993* double cassette.

You're not actually going to do this, are you?

There was never any question. I think it was a Sunday after Christmas, which would make it either Boxing Day in 1993 or the first weekend of 1994. What I'm sure of is that we got it in Woolworths, which was on the ground floor of The Galleries in Bristol until it went bust. Saint Etienne's "You're in a Bad

Way" didn't blow my mind like some of the other songs on these tapes did; forgive me, I was five. But a foundation is a foundation. This album was the hit that got me hooked on hits, patient zero, the first in a population of thousands to be played to death.

I started getting pocket money in 1996, on my eighth birthday, for which I also received a handful of vouchers from aunts and uncles. One of these became item two, *Now That's What I Call Music! 33* double vinyl LP. It came from Virgin Megastore, which took up a massive unit on the first floor of The Galleries. The Galleries is still there, but loads of the shops are now vacant and the Virgin Megastore has become a warehouse for bridalwear. They missed a trick not keeping the name.

I would like to be able to tell a story about how Saint Etienne were there as I began secondary school, as I took my GCSEs and kissed my first boy, but in fact it was twelve years until I bought any more of their records, so they missed all of that. By the time we crossed paths again, I was almost at the end of my second year at university. Item three, *Too Young to Die* vinyl LP. It was, or is, May 2008. Had a dream, woke up, bought a record. This came from Amazon Marketplace, which I think was more of a destination for second-hand vinyl in those days. I had, I suppose, been dreaming about pop music since 1993.

And then the dam was broken. Listen out for the sound of water rushing through, not here — item four, *Sound of Water* vinyl LP (US 2000 pressing), apparently also May 2008, reduced to $8 on the Sub Pop website, given away as an emergency Christmas present years later (see items forty-two and forty-six) — but here, item five, *Finisterre* vinyl LP (UK 2002 pressing), where "Shower Scene" is at the start of side two and there are squalls off the north-west coast of Spain. August 2008. Amazon Marketplace again.

A list of records is a list of places and people coming and going. My parents got the internet in about 2002; it didn't take me long to realise I could buy records off it if I could get my mum to hand over her card details in exchange for the contents of the tin of coins I kept next to my bed. Most of those records came from GEMM, officially the Global Electronic Music Marketplace, which was probably the best database of second-hand vinyl in the world, and like all good things eventually went bankrupt owing a lot of people money. Item six, *Good Humor* vinyl LP (UK 1998 pressing). August 2008. GEMM. Looked like it had been used to sand a wall despite "EX/EX" grading.

Item seven, *Good Humor* vinyl LP (UK 1998 pressing). August 2008. Discogs. No signs of DIY use on this one, but the seller did initially send me the wrong item. Was looking through the list of my old Discogs orders while writing this and I just couldn't believe how cheap everything used to be.

Item eight, *Tiger Bay* vinyl LP (UK 1994 pressing). About October 2008. Prime Cuts, underneath Repsycho in Gloucester Road, Bristol. Buried in one of the two unsorted "indie/dance" crates stowed underneath the main racks in the back room area. Cost about eight quid.

Item nine, "Burnt Out Car" seven-inch single. October 2008. HMV website. The Xenomania mix on the A-side is a classic. No recollection of the B-side, "River", at all.

Item ten, "Like a Motorway" twelve-inch single. Christmas 2008, from my mate Dave. Sleeve had some water damage. Contained four mixes including a great Autechre one. Ultimately has not survived the ruthless culling required to fit all my records in a single house.

Item eleven, "Method of Modern Love" seven-inch single. February 2009. Saint Etienne webstore.

Item twelve, "Method of Modern Love" first CD single. February 2009. Saint Etienne webstore.

Item thirteen, "Method of Modern Love" second CD single. February 2009. Saint Etienne webstore. Signed copies of all three formats were randomly distributed, but not to me.

Item fourteen, *Continental* vinyl LP (Japanese 1997 pressing). June 2009. Came from a shop in Japan called Jet Set, whose website was very reasonably priced. This is the one with the hypothermia girl.

Item fifteen, *Tales from Turnpike House* vinyl LP (UK 2005 pressing). June 2009. Jet Set. The record sounded like breakfast cereal. Seems odd that I didn't buy anything by Saint Etienne in Leeds while I lived there.

Item sixteen, *Built on Sand* CD. September 2009. Discogs. I was now living in a flat with my mate Louise in a semi-derelict part of Ancoats, immediately next door to the internationally famous mega-club Sankeys, which we never visited. We did, however, once fly-tip a Christmas tree in its grounds while drunk. The club is no longer there.

Item seventeen, *Foxbase Alpha* deluxe edition double CD (remastered). About October 2009. The HMV opposite Manchester Victoria station. Already knew the album pretty well because I torrented it while I was a student, along with *Turnpike House*, *Finisterre* and the entire collection of fanclub releases.

Item eighteen, *So Tough* deluxe edition double CD (remastered). Same shopping trip. Got quite ill with the flu (plausibly the one that caused a pandemic) soon after buying these and ended up stranded at David's flat for several days with only the first disc of *So Tough* in my Walkman, maybe as karma for the torrenting.

Item nineteen, *Foxbase Beta* limited edition double CD. October 2009. Saint Etienne webstore. With a couple of exceptions (chiefly "Only Love Can Break Your Heart", which is one of those unassailably perfect records in its original version), I probably like this version of the album better than *Alpha*.

Item twenty, "Only Love Can Break Your Heart" (*Foxbase Beta* mix) twelve-inch single. October 2009 (I think). Piccadilly Records in Oldham Street. Three of the mixes on this are exclusive, one of them by Air France, who I was slightly obsessed with at the time.

Item twenty-one, *So Tough* vinyl LP (UK 1993 pressing). Christmas 2009, from my mum. Seam split on outer sleeve. Disc in really nice condition.

Item twenty-two, *Places to Visit* twelve-inch EP. Some time in 2009 or 2010. Oxfam in Oldham Street, Manchester.

Item twenty-three, *Foxbase Alpha* vinyl LP (UK 1991 pressing). Maybe March 2010. Rooted Records in Bristol. Foxing on inner sleeve.

Item twenty-four, *The Misadventures of Saint Etienne* vinyl LP (1999 Japanese pressing). May 2010. "The Way I Fell for You" is easily a top-five Saint Etienne song, so naturally it was only released on this obscure Japanese soundtrack album.

Item twenty-five, *Finisterre* deluxe edition double CD (remastered). Maybe May 2010. Fopp in Manchester city centre.

Item twenty-six, *Finisterre* DVD. Possibly the same day. Can't find any record at all of where I bought this. Must have been online.

Item twenty-seven, *Tiger Bay* deluxe edition double CD

(remastered). June or July 2010, just before I moved house. Same branch of Fopp.

Item twenty-eight, *What Have You Done Today, Mervyn Day?* CD album. Could have been any time between 2009 and 2012. Kingbee Records in Chorlton. Before I bought a bike, I used to walk the eight-mile round trip to and from Kingbee every time I went, so I didn't have to spend any bus fare that could have been used for records.

Item twenty-nine, *A Glimpse of Stocking* CD album. December 2010. Saint Etienne's Christmas gig at The Ritz, Manchester, which was a listed dance venue just the other side of the canal from our flat at the time. I remember hearing them debut "DJ" at one of these festive shows, but it could have been the year after.

Item thirty, *Design for Today* DVD. 2010 or 2011. Definitely a present from David but can't remember whether it was my birthday or Christmas. BFI collection of short films produced by the Central Office of Information, with two exclusive scores by Saint Etienne. Not really the sort of thing you stick on of an evening, but I did watch it all the way through at the time.

Item thirty-one, "Hobart Paving"/"Who Do You Think You Are" twelve-inch single. 2010 or 2011. Possibly Vinyl Exchange in Oldham Street. Worthwhile for the Aphex Twin mixes, but not so worthwhile that I didn't eventually give it away in a desperate quest for shelf space.

Item thirty-two, "You're in a Bad Way" CD single. I think 2010 or 2011, but can't remember where I got it. It must have been cheap, though, because I only bought it for the little Chris Morris sketch hidden at the end.

Item thirty-three, *Tales from Turnpike House* deluxe edition double CD (remastered). 2010 or 2011. Piccadilly Records in

Oldham Street. I read the interview book while waiting for a haircut at Barberella over the road and can remember the exact moment I learnt that Turnpike House was a real place.

Item thirty-four, *Saint Etienne on 45* seven-inch box set. April 2011. I'd tried and failed to get one at Record Store Day in Manchester, but Steel Wheels in Newcastle had some left over so I think I ordered it over the phone. Maybe a bit of an indulgence at this point but I still really love this little collection.

Item thirty-five, *Xmas '11* seven-inch EP. December 2011. Saint Etienne webstore. Somehow they managed to mount all the sleeves the wrong way round meaning the back cover was sideways.

Item thirty-six, "Tonight" twelve-inch single. Maybe March or April 2012. Most likely Sister Ray in Soho but could have been HMV in Oxford Street or Rough Trade East. I shouldn't have got rid of this — it had an exclusive song from the *Finisterre* soundtrack and a film poster, and strangely now appears to be worth quite a lot.

Item thirty-seven, "I've Got Your Music" twelve-inch single. June or July 2012. Sister Ray in Soho. Wrongly lists an extended version on the A-side, but disappointingly plays the same mix as the album. A proper old-fashioned twelve-inch mix of this would have been brilliant. Ended up in either the Walthamstow High Street Oxfam or the Kingsland Road Oxfam, depending on which of my various desperate culls claimed it.

Item thirty-eight, *Words and Music by Saint Etienne* (UK 2012 pressing). Maybe July 2012. The album came out while I was living out of a suitcase in Clapton, so for the first and only time in my life I wasn't really in a position to buy records. In the end, I think my mum sent it to me as a late birthday present. Unfortunately, it had scratches on both sides and the hole had been drilled so off-centre that if you tried to balance it on your finger it tipped over.

Item thirty-nine, *Tales from Turnpike House* vinyl LP (UK 2005 pressing). July 2012. Flashback in Crouch End. This was an attempt to replace the Japanese purchase with a copy that was playable, but it wasn't a great pressing even without the scratches. Apparently it had previously belonged to Bob Stanley, who lived nearby; it now probably belongs to someone in Margate, because I sold it on to a mate who runs a record shop there when I bought the repress (see item fifty-nine). Wait long enough and everything eventually finds its way back into circulation. Records outlive usefulness and, in the end, they also tend to outlive people. I try not to think about where all of mine will end up.

Item forty, *A London Trilogy* DVD. July 2012. Rough Trade East. Signed by Saint Etienne at an in-store event to promote its release. Paul Kelly and the band had been discussing Geoffrey Fletcher's *The London Nobody Knows* during the Q&A when I swear someone leaning against a pillar raised his hand and said he was Geoffrey Fletcher's son and I think Bob nearly had a heart attack. When I brought this up during an interview for this book, he had no memory of it and now I question the entire episode.

Item forty-one, *Words and Music by Saint Etienne* double CD (US limited edition with bonus album *More Words and Music*). December 2012. Saint Etienne webstore. The site crashed and it took about three hours to buy, which is one of the reasons I refuse to get rid of it, even though I now have a duplicate of the bonus album (see item fifty-six).

Item forty-two, *Sound of Water* vinyl LP (UK 2000 pressing). December 2012. Discogs. To replace the US version I gave away. It turned out the Sub Pop edition sounded significantly better, so this was a rather more generous act than I had intended.

Item forty-three, *Yeah Yeah Yeah: The Story of Modern Pop* paperback by Bob Stanley. October 2013. Amazon. Several years later I was bought a slightly nicer version of this by some mates and lied about not already having it. Surreptitiously gave the original copy to Oxfam.

Item forty-four, *Foxbase Alpha* vinyl LP (UK 1991 pressing). July 2016. Discogs. Better condition than the first copy, though I switched the covers. Part of an endless, doomed attempt to recapture the past in ever higher fidelity as I approached thirty.

Item forty-five, *Home Counties* double vinyl LP. May 2017. Saint Etienne webstore. Wrote a review for the *Islington Gazette* that was misrepresented on the cover of the "Dive" single.[1]

Item forty-six, *Sound of Water* vinyl LP (UK 2017 repress). November-ish 2017. Better than the original UK pressing but probably still not as good as the Sub Pop one.

Item forty-seven, *Foxbase Beta* vinyl LP. December 2018. Saint Etienne webstore. A memory of a memory.

Item forty-eight, *Asleep at the Wheels of Steel* vinyl LP. December 2018. Saint Etienne webstore.

Item forty-nine, *Yeah Yeah Yeah: The Story of Modern Pop* paperback by Bob Stanley. April 2019. Birthday present. Definitely the only copy I have ever owned.

Item fifty, *Lipslide* CD album by Sarah Cracknell. June 2019. Discogs. Added to basket on the eastbound platform

---

[1] My rating was mysteriously upgraded from four stars to five on the cover sticker. Incidentally, the words *Islington Gazette* were printed in much, much smaller writing than *The Guardian*, even though that publication had only given the record three stars, not that I'm bitter.

at Kentish Town West Overground at 10.47pm. What I can't remember is where I had been or why I was drunk.

Item fifty-one, *Words and Music by Saint Etienne* vinyl LP (UK 2020 repress). September 2020. Saint Etienne webstore. Would recommend this over the 2012 pressing.

Item fifty-two, *Interlude* vinyl LP (orange US pressing). September 2020. Discogs. Added to basket during an idle moment at the Hand of Glory in Hackney. By this stage I had finally worked out what this book was going to be about, some four years after it was commissioned. I never regret the records I buy while drunk.

Item fifty-three, *I Love to Paint* vinyl LP. October 2020. Discogs. Part of a desperate rush to fill in the gaps in my collection before I started writing.

Item fifty-four, *Nice Price* double vinyl LP. October 2020. eBay. Quite a lot of hair on the records when they arrived.

Item fifty-five, *Smash Hits 1993* double vinyl LP. October 2020. Discogs. I started thinking seriously about this album again because I was writing a book about how I got into Saint Etienne. My parents eventually got rid of all my tapes, which is fair enough since I left them behind when I moved out in 2006, but I figured it was important to have a copy somewhere. What is a record collection if not a record? For that matter, who in 1993 thought vinyl would outlive cassettes, or that cassettes would stage a sustained if low-level comeback of their own when CDs were on the way out?

Item fifty-six, *More Words and Music by Saint Etienne* vinyl LP (clear splatter edition) and item fifty-seven, *Xmas 2020* CD EP. December 2020. Saint Etienne webstore. The site crashed.

Item fifty-eight, *Sleevenotes* paperback by Bob Stanley. May 2021. London Review Bookshop. *Sleevenotes* had been a very obvious working title for the book you are now reading until I googled it to check whether it had been used.

Item fifty-nine, *Tales from Turnpike House* vinyl LP (UK 2017 repress). May 2021. Rough Trade East. £12.99 in the sale. By far the best-sounding version of this album, ironically also the cheapest of the four I bought.

Item sixty, *I've Been Trying to Tell You* vinyl LP (powder blue UK pressing with bonus CD of remixes). September 2021. Rough Trade East. Saint Etienne, to be frank, threw a bit of a spanner in the works when they announced they had made an album about memory this late in the game, but everything worked out alright in the end.

A list of records is a list of public health disasters. The novel coronavirus made landfall in the UK some time during the months that separated items fifty and fifty-one and, since I managed to drop a swine flu reference way back in item eighteen, I might as well explain that I got Covid at the same time as I got item sixty-one, *Xmas 21* CD EP (UK pressing), in December 2021, though only one of them came from the Saint Etienne webstore. But this is completeness for the sake of completeness. What have I been...

...trying to tell you?

What is a discography if not an autobiography? Why can't the question *what is anyone going to remember this decade for?* be answered? Can you really learn any historical lessons from a list of records? Is there such a thing as living in the moment? Or will we one day be buying remastered copies of albums from 2022 in the hope of recapturing what is now *now*, the stiff neck, the cold air, in ever higher fidelity?

do you remember how saint etienne used saint etienne?

6.

This story cannot end at the end, for the same troublesome reason that it could not begin at the beginning.

Instead, it must end in 2012 — specifically, on May 21, which was an unremarkable Monday during a remarkably wet spring. May 21 2012 was the day that the Saints finally released their eighth album *Words and Music by Saint Etienne*, which makes it the day that this non-linear historiography had always been destined to run out of history.

There are two slightly contradictory reasons for this. The first is that *Words and Music* seems not only to conclude one part of Saint Etienne's career, but to call time on a golden era of British pop music.

By 2012, Saint Etienne had been on the scene for twenty-two years, during which time the record industry had changed almost beyond recognition.

A number of the institutions that had been their platforms, and in whose units their success had been measured, were dead or dying. *Top of the Pops*, which was first broadcast in 1964, had been taken off the air in 2006. Neither *Melody Maker*, whose first issue had pre-dated the existence of the long-playing record, nor *Smash Hits* had survived the Noughties. Even the once unassailable *NME* was struggling for relevance by 2012, having suffered a 50% drop in circulation in just four years.[1]

---

[1] John Reynolds, "Magazine ABCs: *NME* and *Q* Suffer Major Circulation Falls", *Campaign* (August 16, 2012) <https://www.campaignlive.co.uk/article/magazine-abcs-nme-q-suffer-major-circulation-falls/1145894> [accessed January 16, 2022]. The *NME* would cling on to its paid-for print edition until 2015, and a free "brand to hand" version in which little of the magazine's original spirit survived would buy the title a further three years before it became online-only.

Changing algorithms meant groups like St Et who might still have scored a minor hit in 2005 by selling physical copies to a modest but dedicated fanbase were now unable to reach the singles chart at any level, let alone appear in the top forty on a Sunday afternoon. Amazon, iTunes and Spotify had left high street retailers in a state of emergency. Industry heavyweights like EMI and HMV were careering from crisis to crisis and in both cases would be only narrowly rescued from bankruptcy by financial services corporations that had nothing to do with music. Even Croydon's legendary second-hand record shop Beanos had been unable to weather the storm: after implementing a series of cost-cutting measures, it closed in 2009.

There was also some apparent travel in the opposite direction. Vinyl itself had come close to extinction in the Nineties and Noughties but by 2012 the format was enjoying a steady resurgence of interest, fuelled by a captive market who'd missed out first time around. Stranger still, people were starting to sell tapes again. Taxonomies that had once been as normal and as vital as breathing — side one, side two, seven-inch, twelve-inch, *Now That's What I Call Music!* — became quaint nostalgic throwbacks, which was almost worse than if they'd disappeared completely.

Underpinning all of this, even the countercurrent of the vinyl boom, was the digitisation not just of music but of music's consumption, of its communities and criticism. The world that had created Saint Etienne was disappearing. For a time, it seemed that this might not be such a bad thing — that the monopoly once enjoyed by major labels and chain retailers might be replaced by a more equitable model, in which it would be cheaper and easier for musicians to make and distribute music without the prohibitive factors of costly studio time, the whims of A&R suits, and the need to manufacture records and convince shops to stock them. (It could be argued that Spotify snuffed out some of that pluralistic potential by once again centralising music consumption around a single giant corporation whose mathematics favoured bigger artists.) But either way, by 2012, the Saints were no longer playing on home turf.

Words and Music represented two things. It was a last hurrah for some of the institutions that had made Saint Etienne, not all of which had otherwise entirely been forces for good. But it was also a celebration of the human love affair with music for music's sake that would always persist in some form. It was music *about music* — about the thing that Saint Etienne had loved, and remembered loving, so much they'd built their lives around it both professionally and personally.

The record's upcoming release was announced in an email sent to the Saints' fanclub in February 2012. This is what it said:

Do you remember that special alchemy that transforms even the most mundane of experiences — walking home with the headphones on at night, sitting in a bedroom with your friends in the day, getting ready to go out on the weekend — into a lingering moment of seamless enchantment, one that resonates for the rest of your life? Our new album, *Words and Music by Saint Etienne*, is about that. About how music affects your life. How it defines the way you see the world as a child. How it can get you through bad times in unexpected ways.

Maybe this was framed as a question of memory because Saint Etienne no longer used music like this, or maybe it was because, by 2012, music was rarely used like this by *anyone*. Probably a bit of both. Bob, Pete and Sarah would have been interested in the answer not just as music lovers, but also as musicians trying to figure out whether their target audience still actually existed.

This was particularly pertinent in 2012 because *Words and Music* was a record for the fans. It featured a cast of returning favourites and a distillation of all the things that had made the Etienne so great to begin with: persistent melody, evocative storytelling, dry humour, laser-precise (if relatively zeitgeist-blind) arrangements, charming hints of unprofessionalism, light and shade, excess and restraint, reminiscence, a midlife crisis, or three, past and present muddled up, and an intrinsic understanding of what makes a great pop record, what a side one track one should sound like, or a track three, or... It was like a greatest hits LP consisting entirely of new songs, none of which would actually end up being a hit, thanks in part to those updated chart algorithms. Not that it mattered. Just like *Finisterre*, *Words and Music* achieved greatness by returning to something old and making something new.

The second reason we must wrap the story up in 2012 is that *Words and Music* was the moment Saint Etienne ceased in my mind to be a historical group. Since hearing *Too Young to Die*, I had been ravenously acquiring the Saints' existing albums and singles, some of which were nearly as old as I was. But Saint Etienne were a catalogue act to me. They weren't a band that made new stuff.

That changed when *Words and Music* was released, and so did the way I thought about the Etienne as artefacts of the past. While they would continue to work with the fabric of memory, *Words and Music* was the moment I stopped regarding them purely in terms of my *own* memories (real or imagined) of childhood, the time when they had been most active, and began thinking about them as a going concern. *Words and Music*, in other words, was the end of one history and the beginning of another.

Etienne on Etienne

Saint Etienne's return like prodigal children to Jeff Barrett's Heavenly Recordings for *Words and Music*, after transfers to Creation Records, Mantra Recordings and Sanctuary Records, made it seem implausible that they had ever properly left. *Foxbase Alpha* in 1991 hadn't just been Saint Etienne's debut, it had been Heavenly's debut too — the label's first album release, the gospel according to Bob, Pete and Sarah. Surely the Saints and Heavenly had never truly been split up? Even their names were complementary. The fact *Words and Music* was the band's first Heavenly LP since 1994 was no doubt something to do with business, but the reunion could scarcely have been more appropriate given the record's thematic lookback to the group's own golden age.

I should say at this point that Saints are there to be venerated, and so the Etienne had already been referencing themselves for quite some time before the release of *Words and Music*. They began reusing their own lyrics in 2002: a line from "Nothing Can Stop Us" in the middle of "B92" and a quote from Q-Tee's "Filthy" rap (the B-side of "Only Love Can Break Your Heart") on "So Mystified". "How We Used to Live", the nine-minute lead single from *Sound of Water*, lived again in the title of "The Way We Live Now". The ghost of *Foxbase Alpha* lived again through *Finisterre*. And then it lived *again* through *Foxbase Beta*, the remix album they released in 2009. More tower blocks, more watery streets, each time they drew breath.

But *Words and Music* was so accomplished in its self-reference and circular logic as to be Saint Etienne's rational beginning and end, an ouroboric autobiography. *Words and Music* wasn't just knowing — it was subject and object in one.

All of which would have been spectacularly and unlistenably self-indulgent had Saint Etienne not had such a slippery sense of self in the first place and had their stories not also been so widely applicable to the lives of other music lovers. When Sarah says "I", she could really mean anyone. And when she talks about other people, she could just as easily mean herself. All the same, it's pretty obvious that the Saints are the ones haunting *Words and Music by Saint Etienne*.

Let's review the evidence. Item one, the unambiguously self-descriptive album title.

Item two, the story told in the lyrics of the opening track, "Over the Border", about the kids who went "all the way to Somerset just to see Peter Gabriel's house" in the Seventies. Saint Etienne fans have been going all the way to Kentish Town on Tuesday mornings for years just to see Mario's Cafe because of the line "when we meet for a while/ Tuesday morning 10am" in the song of the same name.

Item three, the question mark over what music means as you get older, which is precisely what Saint Etienne and their fans had been doing.

Item four, a song ("Tonight") about going to see your favourite band and discussing what they will play first, just as every Etienne fan surely did when the band went out to tour *Words and Music* weeks after it came out. "Maybe they'll open with an album track, or a top five hit," Sarah exaggerates affectionately in the chorus because of course Saint Etienne have never breached the top ten with a single,[2] never mind the top five.

Item five, a line from that same chorus ("tonight, when the lights are going down, I will surrender to the sound") being quoted nine years later in the film version of *I've Been Trying to Tell You*, which was as clear a hint as any that Saint Etienne themselves had been the thread running through the record.

You're chasing phantoms, she said

In short, *Words and Music by Saint Etienne* is the record collector's *A Christmas Carol*, a one-night trip through the moments of yesterday that tell you about today and tomorrow. In a manoeuvre that is pure Etienne, the Saints become their own Ghosts of Pop Music Past and Pop Music Future, apparitions of the modern world that haunt the English suburbs of the Seventies and Eighties.

The first ghost clears her throat. "When I was ten, I wanted to explore the world," Sarah ventures. Fade in on a small bedroom in Windsor, or Redhill, because — as the group's designated medium — Sarah must channel Bob and Pete's pasts as well. This is the first scene in "Over the Border". She narrates the flashbacks. A nod to "Blue Monday" in the instrumental. The "world atlas" that was *Top of the Pops*. Buying her

---

[2] Except under the name of Cola Boy in 1991, whose dance hit "7 Ways to Love" was recorded without Sarah and, for contractual reasons, fronted publicly by a fictional band made up of the Etienne's mates. It got to number eight. Similarly, "Tell Me Why (The Riddle)", released as "Paul Van Dyk featuring Saint Etienne", made number seven in 2000 during a period of otherwise complete commercial obscurity for the Saints.

first record. The parties, the boys, the exams and, of course, the soundtrack.

Thematically, "Over the Border" is the album's overture — a patchwork of years, a miniature greatest hits within a miniature greatest hits. Each of the remaining tracks on *Words and Music* deals with some single moment given colour and form by pop songs. But as well as memories of music, the record documents memories of expectation.

Words and Music is full of people gearing up to do things or confront situations: "I'm heading for the fair." "Tonight, when the lights are going down, I will surrender to the sound." "I'll get an answer for you soon." "I've got twenty-five years — maybe more if I'm lucky." And most pointedly: "When I was married, and when I had kids, would Marc Bolan still be so important?"

Call it dramatic irony or rhetorical questioning but, by the time this line was written and recorded, it was decades out of date. Both Pete and Sarah actually were married (not to each other) with kids when *Words and Music* was released, living through what had once been only one of a number of possible futures. Marc Bolan's importance had been decided. The question answered itself.

Words and Music memorialised all manner of thrilling and terrifying probabilities in the moments before they were collapsed by time and observation, a bit like "This Is Radio Etienne" immortalised the possibility that Jacques Vendroux might say the wrong thing on tape, because the perishable excitement of virtually every day when you're young is where the magic lies and whence it is lost. But to the teenagers and young adults living those scenes in real-time, the Saints were the maddeningly silent time-travellers who had seen the future, some of which had been and gone without incident, some with bad news, some with good. *Words and Music* was part lullaby, part warning, from their grown-up selves to the children they used to be.

The most striking moments on the album are those in which the boundary between past and present becomes permeable. Only a handful of times do the adult Saints actually speak in their own voices; mostly, they go unnoticed as they rifle through their own heads and surroundings, mind-readers that they have grown to be. On "Over the Border", the refrain of "I'm growing older; heaven only knows what's on its way" intrudes between each cut scene. "Tonight" all but stops dead for eight bars after the second chorus as Sarah reflects: "It's been too long." The final track, "Haunted Jukebox", is even more troubled, pleading at the album's conclusion: "When the record's over/ Just tell me what it's all about." Unlike her chatty companion, the Ghost of Pop Music Future gives nothing away. But the genius of Saint Etienne is the way they use the past to tell stories about the present. And so maybe the answer, or an answer, is all the stories we've already heard, all the corresponding moments of uncertainty and fear and anticipation long since resolved.

June 4 1989

Foxbase Alpha turned eighteen in 2009 and, with no new album to plug, a sort of temporary cottage industry sprang up at Etienne HQ for merchandising the anniversary of their first one. There was a reissue, a tour, a remix album, a T-shirt, even a giant Subbuteo player in the AS Saint-Étienne strip. Maybe all this was the engine for the train of thought that finally led to *Words and Music* three years later — when people like the Saints spend long enough dwelling on their own history, it's to be expected that they might come out with some wonderful esoteric monument to a lost world.

But of course, if you can remember the Eighties, you weren't there. I remember Jon Savage's fugue walk through Camden on June 4 1989, dated and documented in an essay on the back of *Foxbase Alpha*, precisely because I was *not* there. Instead, June 4 1989 has become a numerological lightning rod — with no genuine recollections to compete with, everything in my head that has anything to do with north London gets piled onto it with zero regard for historical accuracy. A recent memory of walking down Camden Road in the snow? Must have been June 4 1989! An unhinged row about Cycle Superhighway 11 that dominated the *Hampstead & Highgate Express* in the latter half of the last decade? I wonder what the Saints thought as they surveyed the planned route on June 4 1989!

June 4 1989 wasn't, in reality, particularly significant even to Jon Savage. He only included that particular date in his liner notes because it was mentioned in the lyrics of *Foxbase Alpha* track "Girl VII", meaning the fugue walk was a false memory even for him. To make matters worse, when writing "Girl VII", Saint Etienne had pulled June 4 1989 out of thin air because it sounded good, meaning the dream sequence lyric in which it appeared ("June 4 1989/ Primrose Hill, Staten Island/ Chalk Farm, Massif Central/ Gospel Oak, São Paolo/ Boston Manor…") was a false memory even for them.

Today, of course, the memories attached to June 4 1989 are mostly memories of either "Girl VII" or Jon Savage's essay, like the Ghost of Pop Music Past keeps returning the members of Saint Etienne to this one date that no one can actually remember anything about. Firstly, *Foxbase Alpha* was re-released in May 2009 with a different, much longer and slightly more factual set of sleevenotes that backgrounded the album's creation. That same May, Saint Etienne played *Foxbase* in full at a handful of anniversary shows, one of which was the first St Et gig I saw (at the Sheffield Leadmill). DJ and producer Richard X, who once gave Liberty X a hit by mashing up Chaka Khan and the Human League, had by this time secured permission to remix the entire *Foxbase Alpha* album, a project that was released as *Foxbase Beta* a few months later. Instead of giving the record yet more sleevenotes, Saint Etienne recorded an audio commentary. Richard X, who is a formalist and perhaps feared that the document of Savage's apocryphal walk would be lost if it was no longer printed on the back cover, recorded Sarah reading out those original liner notes and Fake Sampled the lot over the top of album track "Stoned to Say the Least".

Foxbase Beta did correct one historical injustice. The remixed album restored Stephen Duffy's rightful place on *Foxbase Alpha* by dubbing a single line of his "Fake 88" monologue onto the very end of the final track. *I asked her,* he says again like an old friend, *what is anyone going to remember this decade for? She paused for a second, then said…*

By this point I'm not sure anyone knows which decade we're even talking about any more and, anyway, the only answer to have survived the edit is "waffle cardigans" — evidently, everything else on Stephen's giant original list (items two to forty-three) would not prove so memorable after all.

No vinyl version of *Beta* was released in 2009; the format was in slow recovery from its 2007 sales nadir and demand was still tiny compared with the market for digital formats. That was to change, and with it the business case for what remains a costly, complicated product to manufacture, to the extent that by 2018 it made monetary sense to press a thousand copies of *Foxbase Beta* on vinyl. For this release, Richard X wrote yet another set of sleevenotes, an essay reflecting on both *Foxbase Alpha* and *Foxbase Beta*, which had by then become an archive recording of its own — a memory of a memory of a memory of nothing.

The original *Foxbase*, whatever it was, and the events of June 4 1989, whatever they were, retreated further and further into the distance. Yet they remained present, recalled and repro-duced each time we stepped outside the frame. Unfortunately, by 2018, the words "waffle cardigans" had also been deleted from Stephen's memory (item one becomes item zero), leaving a dangling open quote mark at the end of the LP, perhaps an invitation to supply your own answers or simply to flip the record over again by way of response.

How can it be that I was watching Saint Etienne tour *Foxbase* barely a year after dreaming about *Too Young to Die*? The fact is that, in those short months, I had gone from ingenue to connoisseur, overwriting a recent past in which I had unfor-givably little idea of who Saint Etienne were with the far more plausible and less negligent memory of having loved them my whole life, or at least since June 4 1989. Saint Etienne are both productive and withholding, and they probably make all their fans feel like this.

Sarah: What happens is you put a record out and then, once it's out and you've done the tour, you just don't listen to it again at all. Why would you sit there and listen to your own records? So when they come up — when we've done our big fancy boxsets and then we'll get new sleevenotes — I go back and listen to the record again. I'm always pleasantly surprised about how much better they are than I thought they might be, basically! I guess also, because it's a few years later, they sound a little bit naive in places, or you feel like maybe we're slightly better songwriters than we were then or something — but the naivety is really charming. Maybe not to everyone, but to me it seems quite charming.

Who's been trying to tell you?

There is a sort of are-they-aren't-they about the young people at the centre of Saint Etienne's 2021 album and film *I've Been Trying to Tell You* and whether or not they represent the young Saints, which mirrors the probability that the record does or doesn't refer to the years 1997 to 2001, from which most of its samples are drawn. Admittedly, the dates are out — because, by 1997, the Saints had made three albums and were in their thirties swanning around Europe rather than teenagers playfighting beside the Thames — but perhaps in this project the Nineties are a metaphor for the Eighties, Natalie Imbruglia a metaphor for Grandmaster Flash, or perhaps the young people represent youth at large, and how could Saint Etienne write about youth in the abstract but through their own charming, naive youth?

Saint Etienne's film career may have been inevitable but few would have guessed in 1990 that they would one day wind up putting their own lyrics into the mouths of actors who weren't even born when they came out — few, perhaps, except Saint Etienne themselves, who always seemed to be writing with a future in mind. Each of the lyrics quoted in *I've Been Trying to Tell You* (these pieces of self-referential dialogue are omitted from the album and only appear in the movie) is a giant nod to the audience watching the film at the expense of the characters' agency, like a night-time dream concocted from conversations heard during the day, or the moment the star of a metafictional novel becomes aware of their own lack of free will. You've got one lad asking another: "Did you see the KLF last night?" Later, another character says: "Only love can mend a broken heart," which is a line from the 1993 B-side "Paper" that reverses the rather more familiar title of the Saints' first single "Only Love Can Break Your Heart". These lines seem a bit like nonsense because the references are so out of place. But the Saints are only doing what they've always done: cutting up their memories, using the clash between past and present to send up the classics with the same poignant, self-deprecating good humour they've always had.

Memorials to remembering

My grandma died on March 11 1995, leaving my mum a pile of old diaries dating back to the Fifties.

My mum, in a mixture of grief and curiosity, was thus able to fast-forward her way through thousands of weeks of my grandma's life in quite granular detail. I found this elevation of the everyday into a kind of sacred text fascinating. It was not a coincidence that I started keeping a diary of my own a few years later.

If I think about January 1 1998 now, all I can really remember is writing that first entry in an uncharacteristically neat hand, like I had someone to impress.

But the business of memory changed significantly between January 1 1998 and December 31 2017, the day I stopped writing.

Aside from her bank account, my grandma had no digital footprint. Her diaries are the primary archive of her life. If I died tomorrow, I would leave behind video messages, newspaper columns, a DIY album recorded with two mates in my parents' spare room, two books, thousands of stupid tweets, a last.fm, a Facebook page, a Discogs account, an Instagram.

You might sensibly ask why I kept a diary for so long. It was occasionally therapeutic to process my present day into tomorrow's history, sometimes while drunk or high or half-asleep, but 90% of the time it seemed more like a millstone. I began to feel that nothing had really happened until I wrote it down, that the empty pages that frequently built up were debts to settle. I was holding on to an outdated idea of memory, an archive of the idea of an archive, an image of a stranger rifling through a drawer and fast-forwarding through a past that was already documented.

My grandpa died on March 1 1995, leaving my mum a temperamental mid-Eighties record player that my parents set up in my room. This is known as "creating a monster".

The discovery that it wasn't just old people's music that came on vinyl was very exciting to me. It was like being seven years old and suddenly being told you were allowed to drive a fire engine. I realise it sounds dull, when other kids were dreaming about Power Rangers and Bristol Rovers, that I was dreaming about filling a small shelving unit with albums so I could be like my mum, or imagining that anyone might one day find my shelves as fascinating and fundamental as I found hers.

But the business of listening to pop songs has also changed significantly since my grandparents died. Nobody will ever experience my record collection in the way I experienced my mum's because access to music is quite sensibly no longer constrained by physical ownership. Records may look the same as they did then, but their meaning is different. They are no longer so universal, so recognisable, as they were in 1995.

Music no longer necessarily looks like the spines of album covers lined up on a shelf.

So now when I buy records, I guess it is a memorial to a defunct form of remembering, an archive of the idea of an archive.

Saint Etienne understand that it isn't just the artefacts of the present that change, but also the ways we collect and recall them. Like diaries and records, *Words and Music by Saint Etienne* is an archive of the idea of an archive. It is a work of folk memory, or pop memory, a series of stories that only make sense if you remember for a moment how we used to use and how we used to remember music in the twentieth century. Kids in this world have their music rationed. They spend weeks saving up for an album on the strength of one single. Boys and girls swap records. A date is a lad on the doorstep with a handful of CDs. We tape songs off the top forty and pile the cases on every available surface: TDK, Memorex, Maxell. When something is gone, it's gone. There is no ledger. You will tune in to the radio halfway through a song and have no way of knowing what it is. When my friends' kids grow up and write books about music, what aspects of the present day will have stuck with them? What unremarkable realities from the early part of this decade will be sources of nostalgia and myth, grief and curiosity, in twenty-five years?

They too will no doubt experience the curious clash of remembered anticipation with the reality of the thing itself, just like the time I visited Mario's Cafe on a Tuesday morning in 2012; the overlaying of my mum's record collection with the reality of the albums on my own shelves; my grandma's diaries and the fact of my own, stuffed into a plastic box with a folding lid that I keep under the bed.

Sarah: It's interesting having kids, because the things that they listen to and the way that they listen to it is very different. They just have so much access to anything and everything, whereas when I was at their age it was about clans. You would meet people and they would introduce you to something that you couldn't find on the radio or TV. You could only find it if you met certain people and you went to a record shop and you bought it. And that felt really special, but I do think the way my kids find music still feels special to them — it's just easier. And they can mix it up a lot more. They listen to old things, they listen to everything.

I blew two hundred quid of my student loan on a job lot of mid-Nineties *Now* compilations in 2007. The records turned up about a week later in a cheap laminated case that had been wrapped in parcel tape. My housemates all thought I was crazy.

I can scarcely remember ever having wanted something so much. I suppose I was going through a sort of quarter-life crisis weaponised by the novelty of having a bank account into which the government deposited £1,000 three times a year. I was nineteen but in a sense, in the moment that I bought them, I was a kid again.

Only a handful of shops in the centre of Bristol were still selling vinyl by the mid-Nineties. I vividly remember the release of each *Now* album, and the niche, incommunicable excitement of seeing the covers blown up to twelve inches. *Now 33* was the only one I could afford to buy, having just had a birthday, but I wanted them all. In particular, I was *desperate* to get *Now 34* on vinyl for Christmas in 1996, but it couldn't be tracked down by the time December came around (it had been released in August).

I can't remember why, more than a decade later, I was searching eBay for the words *Now That's What I Call Music*. I guess I must have been caught off guard by a memory, dredged up by some random synaptic event, triggered by the air or the light. And there they were, spread out on someone's floor for a low-res photoshoot, waiting for a buyer dumb or romantic enough to deserve them. If I say it was like a dream you will have to believe that this is the sort of thing I dream about. Seeing them on the shelf, even now, feels emotional in a way I don't think I can put into words.

Bob: When I was a kid, I got the Shadows' *Twenty Golden Greats*. It was a best-of and I knew maybe two or three of the songs on it and then the rest of it was all new to me and I loved it. But it had an inner sleeve with their other albums that you could buy and I always wanted one called *The Sound of the Shadows*. The cover is — it's got this odd Thirties lettering with their cut-out heads. It's a cheap but evocative sleeve. And eventually someone bought it for me as a present when I was in my thirties and that was like — well, my heart was going back to when I was eleven years old and I really wanted this record, and it felt like quite an emotional thing, even though someone was just buying me an album by the Shadows for my birthday.

All of this grief and curiosity is to say that memories of music build up. Time deposits them in layers, one for each spin, each dream in the streets or the sheets. Which isn't to say the layers at the bottom can't still be felt: sometimes strata that have been pushed further down make marks on the surface indelible like fairy rings or destructive like lava just because the timbre of a particular guitar sound or the movement of a bassline against a chord change catches you off guard this one time, and before you know it you're crying at "So Pure" by Baby D, a song that no one was ever meant to cry at.

That was how I used to think about the geology of memory, anyway. The very bottom layer in each cross-section was the first time you heard a certain record and the deposits higher up were all the more recent ones. Maybe it goes like this: you see it on *Top of the Pops* (layer one); you buy the single (layer two) and it survives about a month on heavy rotation before the tape starts to get mangled and develops imperfections that even years later you will never fully be able to un-hear (layer three); you get the album for Christmas (layer four); you're listening to the album on a coach to somewhere feeling excited or anxious or bored as you stare out the window (layer ten); you meet a boy at uni who has the same records you bought as a kid and it makes you long for home but also for him (layer thirty); you hear the song at a club, the album is reissued, you see the band on stage, and on and on and on you go remembering the last layer, and the first.

But what about all those memories of *not* knowing the song that lurk even further down? The first records I bought had taken months to save up for, 50p a week, a figure on a little whiteboard by the door edging glacially towards £12.99, and I thought about those records *a lot* before I was actually able to bring them home and play them. One of my strongest memories of *Now 33*, the one that got us into this mess, is of standing at the bus stop in the chilly sunshine, sliding the album out of the bag and trying to understand that it was mine, like the feeling of completing a video game, studying the back, noticing the songs I already knew, but also the songs I didn't. The memory of that record being unfamiliar barely makes sense to me when I know it so well, but the image is there all the same.

I have so many memories of standing at that bus stop and trying to imagine what the record I was taking home might sound like — no matter what shop I'd been to, what the record was, what century it was, whether I was on my own or with my mum or with my mates, the colour of the sky, time of year, time of life, the journey home involved standing in pretty much that exact spot looking across the dual carriageway towards the back of Debenhams, or, if you faced to the right, down The Haymarket towards Rupert Street. (If you'd faced left, you wouldn't have seen the bus coming.)

Maybe it will already have gone like this: you sit on the bed and take the record out of its cover for the first time (layer zero). You get the bus into town. You see it advertised on TV. In those leaflets for record clubs that they used to give out. In the hands of other shoppers or kids at school. You become aware that a record exists — maybe in a shop, maybe because of those "new release" postcards that record companies used to put through the door. Each of the times you thought about those things as you dropped a coin into a tin or zoned out during double PE on a Wednesday afternoon. For some of those *Now* albums, sheepishly bought off an internet auction website in the mid-Noughties, the imagined reality of owning and hearing them had been collecting layers for well over a decade. And now, when I take any of them down off the shelf, all those stratified memories are screaming back at me in various combinations like harmonics, back to the day when, as a kid, I first picked up the record cover and tried to memorise the tracklisting before reluctantly putting it back in the rack for someone else to buy. Each subsequent play sounds like those predictions of how it would sound before it even sounds like itself. In the instantaneous present, there is no music, only the memory of the beat just gone and the wait for the next. What did Bob imagine Jacques Vendroux was going to say when he pressed the "record" button on that day back in 1990 or 1991 (layer zero)? Does he remember not knowing?

Bob: I was working in a record shop when *Now 3* and *Now 4* came out and, as I said before, '83 to '86 I think of just being a bit of a void, really, so all the early *Nows* — the ones that people are generally most attached to — I don't really like. I just don't like the music on them. The ones I like the most are the early Nineties ones, I suppose.

K-Tel Records were around before *Now* existed, which makes me sound like I'm from the war or something, but those were the first records I had — or at least my parents had, and Pete's parents had. Quite garish sleeves and low production values, but they were important to me. Everyone on there had to be important — I was seven years old. I thought, surely you had to be important or you wouldn't be on something called *20 Dynamic Hits*. I think a lot of people bought those things just to stick on at dinner parties or drinks parties in the background. I still hear those records in sequence and that's how I know those songs — I still think of Chicory Tip and Sly and the Family Stone and Olivia Newton-John and Dandy Livingstone in the same thought, because they were cheek by jowl on this K-Tel album.

It's kind of a surprise that there wasn't a song on *Words and Music* about compilations, particularly since Bob Stanley frequently gets interviewed about them. The closest thing was "Haunted Jukebox", the track that inspired this book, which dissects through a series of flashbacks the way memories get trapped inside music and then released upon impact with the needle of the record player whether you want them or not.

Of course, that also makes "Haunted Jukebox" the most reflexive song on *Words and Music* — it has itself become haunted, impossible to hear without remembering the day David left for Japan, or the weeks that followed. "The spirit's in the air," it laments. "It's like the tunes are everywhere I want to go." (This isn't entirely true — the likelihood of hearing a 2012 Saint Etienne album track in the wild is extremely slim — but "Haunted Jukebox" is one of my favourite songs so it's unavoidable in that sense.) Observation collapses uncertainty. So, too, the Ghost of Pop Music Present hands *Words and Music* over to the Ghost of Pop Music Past the moment the record finishes, and the album that retold Saint Etienne's history becomes a chapter in its own tale.

Since I've remembered I'm trying to make a point, item six, *Words and Music* features at least two former members of Xenomania, the production house co-founded by "He's on the Phone" mixmaster Brian Higgins in the late Nineties. And since I'm pointedly trying to make Saint Etienne remember, item seven, the little instrumental hook at the very end of "Haunted Jukebox", which is what you might call a *haunted* version (grainy, incomplete, upside-down) of the piano loop that runs through the intro and the verses of "He's on the Phone", the countersign I talked about in the first chapter. It's easier if I show you:

He's on the Phone

Haunted Jukebox

Haunted phone box

In other words, the end of this story is an approximate mirror image of the beginning. Layer n contains the memory of layer one. Not that the hook in "He's on the Phone" would actually have been there in the first place without Higgins' intervention.

Bob: I remember Brian Higgins driving up to my flat at four or five in the morning with the finished version of "He's on the Phone" — because he still had a day job working for a book publisher. He'd been working on it and he drove up from East Grinstead to north London in the middle of the night and said: "I've done it — I've finished it. I want to play it to you now." Rang on the doorbell.

I thought it was amazing. He was going: "What you've done there is you've written the hook, the main hook, and you've just stuffed it on the end of the song, that's ridiculous, I'm going to bring it to the beginning of the song," and I was like: "Yeah, you're right, you're absolutely right, of course." It was great, it was really exciting. It was one of those things where — I think we thought if it wasn't a hit we probably would have split up. I remember opening the door and him standing there like an excited puppy. I remember that so well, it's etched in my memory.

Saint Etienne advertised *Words and Music* as a record about how music shaped people's lives, which is what Saint Etienne, Heavenly and Xenomania had all been doing both collectively and individually for a number of years by that point, making it into a sort of joint autobiography, or at least a biography of the people who loved Saint Etienne, Heavenly and Xenomania. Among those people were the songwriters and producers Tim Powell and Nick Coler, who had worked with the Saints on *Finisterre*, *Turnpike* and a handful of singles before quitting Xenomania in 2010. Notable by his absence was Brian Higgins himself, whose shadow hangs over the record that sounds so much like his work and features several of his old collaborators.

I wonder if "He's on the Phone" is one of Bob's haunted singles — a stratified memory that begins with A&R maverick Steve Allen introducing the Saints to Higgins, and ends with Bob and the others parting ways with Xenomania, the outfit Higgins had co-founded, whose obsessive quest for the pop singularity was perhaps a case of the perfect being the enemy of the good.

The more I think about it, the more natural it seems that I should have discovered "He's on the Phone", and therefore Saint Etienne themselves, through a "various artists" compilation. The song never appeared on a studio album. Instead it is nomadic, popping up on St Et's own compilations one after another in various edits (*Too Young to Die*, *Casino Classics*, *Continental*, *Smash the System*, *Travel Edition*, *London Conversations*), which is the case for a number of the Saints' best-known singles, thanks to their apparent dual instincts of intentional obscurity and continuous self-reappraisal — in other words, a fuck you to the cult of the LP as the beginning and end of music.

As early as the limited edition *You Need a Mess of Help to Stand Alone*, which came out as a bonus CD with *So Tough* in 1993, the Saints were framing and reframing their one-offs and outtakes within rarities collections, best-ofs, remix albums, and slightly odd hybrids like *Continental*, never really settling for a finished history but using the artefacts of the past to tell a story about who Saint Etienne were *now* and how they'd got there, like the way they sampled records from every decade imaginable to tell a story about the Nineties when that decade had barely got under way. Maybe that's partly about the process of signing to a succession of new labels, each of which wanted a slice of the back catalogue, but it's also about the Saints' identity shifting, about their natural ability to turn old material into something new, because these sets were never cut-price cash-ins: they always had new sleevenotes, new songs, obvious attention paid to the tracklisting, immaculate artwork, multiple formats, and so on.

The most extreme example is the song "Angel", which is so edgy as perhaps to have no definitive version at all. It was planned as a single in 1996 but abandoned because the Saints got cold feet about it; two very different remixes of the track by Way Out West and Broadcast were nonetheless released on *Casino Classics*, then re-released on *Continental* and *Smash the System*, before the seven-minute original mix (which may or may not have been the track they had once intended to release) was included on the fanclub-only *Nice Price* collection in 2006. Is there anything so dreary, so cut and dried, as a canon? Far more interesting to have a shifting body of work to forget, discover, remake, nothing sacred but everything eligible for beatification.

That's what I call Words and Music

One of the most charming things about those Nineties compilations is their, well, now-ness: though it was already part of a series with nearly three dozen instalments, nothing about *Now 33* looks inward or backward and there is no indication, even at a time when the record industry thought itself indestructible, that the brand expected to live to a hundred, which it has. The continued existence of *Now* compilations is itself a memorial to a defunct form of remembering, to an era before the obsessive recycling of old pop music year after year: EMI didn't expect, I don't think, that anyone would pay a couple of hundred pounds for a set of them in 2007, much less the far higher prices they command today.

In recent years, the custodians of the *Now* series have finally cottoned on, and the brand has ramped up the business of eating itself, churning out multi-format reissues and tacking selections from the earliest albums onto the ends of some of the most recent ones — *Now 104* concludes with a few "throwback" tracks from *Now 4*, for instance. *Now 100* was the collection's own *Words and Music*, a sort of *Now That's What I*

Call Now That's What I Call Music!, *Now* multiplied by *Now*, in that it contains the largest amount of self-reference, its entire second disc devoted to a run-down of the "greatest" tracks from the series' thirty-five-year history,[3] with the long-retired pig logo wheeled back out for the front cover, remastered, remembered, part of an endless, doomed attempt to recapture the past in ever higher fidelity. Perhaps one day each *Now* album will have the same tracklisting as the one before it. Do you remember what we used to call music? Do you remember how we used to remember?

The history of Saint Etienne is the history of *Now* compilations, because these were the circumstances under which I "discovered" Saint Etienne,[4] and while the Saints' own history does not begin with *Now 33* or end with *Words and Music*, a sort of *Now That's What I Call Saint Etienne!*, Saint Etienne multiplied by Saint Etienne, they are the only places I could have begun or ended this history of remembering. Over the course of *Words and Music*, Saint Etienne cycle through childhood into the present day, forty-eight minutes to get from "when I was ten" to "when the record's over," just at the exact moment that it is. *Words and Music* catches up to itself like *Now 100*. No surprise that I dreamed about *Too Young to Die* in the months after buying all those *Now* albums. I was catching up to myself. It was my *Sound of the Shadows*, an album that should have belonged to a much younger version of me but that, by some error of the universe, I'd never actually got round to hearing. If I want to understand Saint Etienne, I am the last person I should ask. The first people I should ask are the ones who put them on side four of *Now 33*.

---

[3] Reader, they are not.

[4] Sort of. See above.

Ashley Abram, Now That's What I Call Music! compiler from Now 2 to Now 81:

I suppose the main thing is that it only just made it onto the album — the single was briefly in the top twenty towards the end of 1995, so would have been a little dated by the time our compilation was released in late March the following year. The backers of *Now*, at that time EMI/Virgin/PolyGram, would always be lobbying for their own tracks to be included ahead of "outside" ones, so I seem to recollect that they said: "This track is too old and wasn't in the chart for very long — we want one of ours instead."

However, I felt it was a good single and well worth a place on the album. So I guess you could say you might not have heard of Saint Etienne until a later date — or maybe never at all — if the track hadn't been included!

Alright, maybe this wasn't such a smart question to ask. Then again, maybe the key to understanding Saint Etienne is all of the nearly-didn'ts: that we nearly didn't use them to live, that the whole thing could have been avoided, like Jacques Vendroux and his unscripted monologue, an accidental hit, a pack of jokers, a light under a bushel, a house of dreams, a heavenly avenue. And maybe the reason I can't shake them off is the fact that some of the nearly-didn'ts were mine.

A scene from a film circa 1996. We caught the bus down Cheltenham Road en route for The Galleries. I could have spent my birthday money on anything.[5] One wrong move and there'd have been no Blur, no Radiohead, no Lush, no Pulp, no Dubstar, no

---

[5] Well, not *anything*. The only thing I ever wanted was pop music. But I remember that I briefly considered buying a Simply Red album instead.

Saint Etienne. Fortunately, I hadn't been briefed. I didn't realise I was making a decision that would shape so much of my future. The cover looked right, the LP was in stock, the sun was out. That was enough.

Ashley Abram had a final run-in with Sarah Cracknell before he retired. She'd provided vocals for Mark Brown on "The Journey Continues" at the end of 2007. It became a moderate crossover hit in Britain and, accordingly, scraped onto *Now 69* in thirty-sixth place — a promotion! — straight after "Something Good 08", the unexpected (and short-lived) Utah Saints comeback.

The two sets of Saints had crossed over before, way back in the tracklisting of *Smash Hits 1993*. Maybe it was some elaborate calculus that kept putting the same bands in the same positions. Maybe this was how Ashley Abram amused himself. Maybe it was a memorial of sorts to the time he'd managed to get all three members of Saint Etienne on one *Now* album.

Whatever his motives, Abram (unlike Jacques Vendroux) always seemed to know exactly what he was doing — every choice of track, every choice of edit, echoing through pop music history at thirty-three revolutions a minute.

Perhaps, without "He's on the Phone", I'd have come across the Saints somewhere else. Or, perhaps, without the countersign of that song at that moment (I'm making an educated guess that it was April 20 1996, the first Saturday after my birthday), their smart, lonely brand of pop music, distant but impulsive, past as present and present as past, wouldn't have made sense when I heard it. Maybe I'd have tried to write a book about *Now* compilations. Maybe I wouldn't have written anything at all without the Etienne and their ongoing assault on my subconscious, whose reliably unreliable drip drip drip will always wake me up in 2008, back where it all began, dreaming about the other places it all began. Perhaps all those turnings I nearly missed, records I nearly didn't buy, dreams I nearly didn't have, are the answer when Saint Etienne ask on "Join Our Club" if you believe in magic. What is anyone going to remember this decade for? Ever since Ashley Abram smuggled them onto side four, shoes in hand, it's been kind of obvious.

Acknowledgements

A lot of people were very patient about this book. Tariq Goddard at Repeater waited four years for me to start writing it. The saintly Josh Turner and the design and marketing teams waited a further year for me to stop sending them tedious minor edits. Bob Stanley, Pete Wiggs and Sarah Cracknell were extremely kind about all my pestering and generous with their time. My long-suffering husband David listened to me droning on about it endlessly for most of 2021. So did my amazing friends Ned Simons and Jess Brammar. Paul English, who blogs about compilation albums at apopfansdream.wordpress.com, put me in touch with Ashley Abram, who was very nice about the silly questions I asked him. Dimitar Bankov was happy for me to refer to his fascinating work on word use in pop songs. John Stoddart was kind enough to let us use his stunning band photograph on the cover. Rob McNicol provided some dreadfully helpful comments on an early version of chapter four. Sam Gelder, Chris Bailey and Nick Perry helped me find and understand the data on social homes lost and social homes built. My mates Iain Gardner and Anthony Schrag invited me to stay in their beautiful flat in Edinburgh while I tried to finish the first draft and had a totally predictable meltdown.

Obviously, though, this book is for my mum.

Repeater Books

is dedicated to the creation of a new reality. The landscape of twenty-first-century arts and letters is faded and inert, riven by fashionable cynicism, egotistical self-reference and a nostalgia for the recent past. Repeater intends to add its voice to those movements that wish to enter history and assert control over its currents, gathering together scattered and isolated voices with those who have already called for an escape from Capitalist Realism. Our desire is to publish in every sphere and genre, combining vigorous dissent and a pragmatic willingness to succeed where messianic abstraction and quiescent co-option have stalled: abstention is not an option: we are alive and we don't agree.